TOP 20 SKITS
for youth ministry

Chris and Sue Chapman

Group

Loveland, Colorado
www.group.com

Dedication

For our parents
Nanna and Poppa, Grandma and Granddad

Top 20 Skits for Youth Ministry

Visit our website: **group.com**

Credits
Acquisitions Editor: Kate S. Holburn
Editor: Alison Imbriaco
Creative Development Editor: Mikal Keefer
Chief Creative Officer: Joani Schultz
Copy Editor: Lyndsay Gerwing
Book Design and Production: Toolbox Creative
Cover Art Director: Jeff A. Storm
Cover Designer: Veronica Lucas
Production Manager: Dodie Tipton

Unless otherwise indicated, all Scripture quotations are taken from the *Holy Bible*, New Living Translation, copyright © 1996, 2004. Used by permission of Tyndale House Publishers, Inc., Wheaton, Illinois 60189. All rights reserved.

Library of Congress Cataloging-in-Publication Data
Chapman, Chris, 1957-
  Top 20 skits for youth ministry / Chris and Sue Chapman.
    p. cm.
  Includes index.
  ISBN-13: 978-0-7644-3113-5 (pbk. : alk. paper)
 1. Church work with teenagers. 2. Drama in Christian education. 3.
Comedy sketches. I. Title: Top twenty skits for youth ministry. II.
Chapman, Sue, 1960- III. Title.
  BV1485.C52 2006
  246'.72-dc22

ISBN 978-0-7644-3113-5
0-7644-3113-7

10 9 8 7 6 5 4   15 14 13 12 11 10
Printed in the United States of America.

Table of Contents

Introduction

Welcome to *Top 20 Skits for Youth Ministry!*

In these pages, you'll find 20 dramatic stories that will involve your kids in lessons you want them to learn. Use these skits to capture their attention and to engage them as you introduce big topics and big ideas.

Using stories to teach is fun. It's flexible. But as much as we'd like to claim it was our idea, the fact is that someone else got there first.

Jesus taught through parables, which are dramatic stories to make a point. It's an outstanding technique (we did mention that Jesus used it, didn't we?) and one you'll use as you and your group perform these totally non-lame, non-cheesy, non-slick short plays.

If your youth group isn't particularly sold on doing skits, these are the skits that will change their minds. These skits help build faith, connect with the great themes of the Bible, and set the stage for fun—all at the same time.

The historical and cultural contexts of Bible accounts often make it hard for teenagers to fully appreciate the relevance and poignancy of biblical issues and events. These skits help clarify events so the gospel comes through loud and clear. Your young people themselves become an active part of the teaching/learning process. They will perform, discuss, and watch as the skits speak to them about a God who loves them, about people past and present who have experienced that love, and about a very personal relationship with God.

But wait, there's more! Every skit is easy to present; complex scenery, sets, or props are not needed. Many have those useful "extra" roles (with few or no lines) so you can include everyone who wants to be in the skit. And each skit includes the following:

> **"And the Moral of the Story Is…"**—a handy list of themes and issues the skit touches on that are eminently discussable.

> **"Program Blurb"**—a quick summary of the main action of the skit so you can see at a glance what it deals with.

> **"What God Says"**—a series of relevant Bible verse references that tie in with the action of the skit and the discussion themes.

> **"Handy Info"**—some background information and thoughts about discussion issues.

> **"Props and Wardrobe"**—a list of what you'll need (all very simple and inexpensive, of course).

> **"Stage Manager's Clipboard"**—details about any setting-up type things that need to be done.

"Cast List"—includes special features of personalities to make it easier to cast and perform the roles.

"Strain Your Brain, and Stretch Your Faith"—discussion questions and suggested activities to get people really learning and grappling with big ideas.

And the whole thing comes with a cool CD. This CD has both sound effects and fun labels and signs you can use to enhance your performance. Whenever you see the CD icon, you'll know you can fire up your performance with one of these extras. Icons with track numbers mean you'll find sound effects to use. PDF icons mean you can find signs and labels to help you involve the audience in the action.

Use these skits in your youth group meetings. Discuss the background. Deal with the themes. Enjoy the fun—but don't miss the learning.

Consider performing a skit your group knows well in a church service. Connect it to what your pastor is dealing with in the sermon. Your group will learn through discussing the skit and its themes, and they'll help the larger congregation grow.

At outdoor settings, youth camps, retreats, and concerts, these skits can be a powerful way for members of your group to share their faith with non-Christian audiences.

So
what are you waiting for?
Jump in!

Leader Guide to Frightening Stage Terms

OK, we admit it. This book contains stage directions to prevent actors and actresses from falling off the stage, running into the wings, and so on. They are abbreviated with letter combinations such as SR, DSL, and USR. They sound scary, but they are actually very easy.

First, everything is from the actor's point of view:

SR (stage right) is the side of the stage to the right of actors looking at the audience.

Upstage (US) is away from the audience. (It's what the uneducated masses call "the back of the stage"—how primitive!)

Downstage (DS) is toward the audience.

CS is **center stage**, or in the middle.

These initials allow handy combinations. For example, **CSL** is **center stage left**, or in the middle but to the left of an actor facing the audience.

DSR is **downstage right**, or toward the audience and on the actor's right.

See how it works?

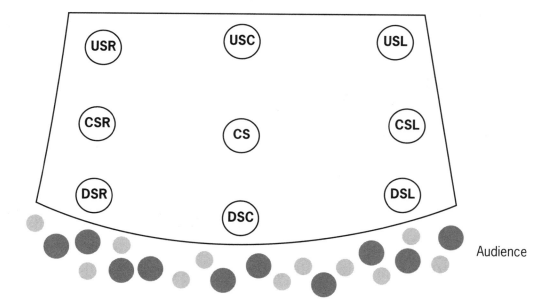

USR (upstage right)   USC (upstage center)   USL (upstage left)

CSR (center stage right)   CS (center stage)   CSL (center stage left)

DSR (downstage right)   DSC (downstage center)   DSL (downstage left)

The Messiah Doll

And the Moral of the Story Is…
the Crucifixion, grace, Jesus' mission, human nature, obedience

Program Blurb:

The "Children of Israel" are waiting for the big present—the Messiah. They have plans for exciting games to play with the Messiah. But they discover that the Messiah doesn't have a control panel and, instead, does things they didn't expect.

What God Says:

Matthew 11:28-30; Matthew 18:1-4; Mark 8:31-37; Luke 6:27-28; Luke 14:27

Handy Info:

The Jews of the first century had been invaded by Assyrians (see 2 Kings 15:19-20 and 17:3-4), Babylonians (see 2 Kings 25:1-12), and Romans (see Luke 3:1)—and they were sick of being a conquered people. They were avidly looking forward to the coming of the cosmic figure (see Jeremiah 33:14-16 and Luke 1:67-75) who would restore their kingdom, kick out the Romans, punish all the sinners, and usher in a golden age.

Many Jews believed that the Messiah would be introduced by the return of Elijah (see Malachi 4:5-6 and Matthew 11:7-14). (Like Elijah, John the Baptist was a "wilderness man." Check out Matthew 3:4 and 2 Kings 1:8 to compare their taste in clothes.) The Jews felt confident that the Messiah would be an unbeatable military hero—a superhero in every sense.

So Jesus entered a highly charged political atmosphere in which many people were ready to get the Messiah going. However, the kingdom of God that he announced was very different from what people expected.

God isn't tame and predictable. In fact, he often works in unexpected ways.

Props and Wardrobe:

You'll need a few garden rakes, feather dusters, and shovels. John the Baptist and Jesus should wear period biblical robes, and John the Baptist should have a leather belt and staff. The Children can be in modern or period clothes.

Stage Manager's Clipboard:

You'll need a stage with wings or screens to hide characters when they exit. Actors can mime being dunked in the Jordan River. (However, your group may want to channel a real river through the auditorium and across the stage.)

Cast List: **Children of Israel (Child 1, 2, 3, 4, and 5):** mixed group of elementary school–age children, still young enough to look forward excitedly to presents. Children 2 and 4 are girls. Children 1, 3, and 5 are boys.

John the Baptist: prophetic figure

Jesus: the "Messiah doll" who refuses to be a doll and does his own thing

Voice-Over: a strong narrator voice

Cue: For Jesus, choose an actor who can freeze in position to suggest that he is an action figure.

Set the CD to track 1, which provides the sound of a hostile crowd and then of nails being driven into wood. Start the CD as Jesus walks off the stage.

The Messiah Doll

Voice-Over: And here are the Children of Israel! They're excited because they know the present they've been waiting for will arrive soon.

(Children of Israel race onstage from both sides. They are excited and rush around chattering about "present time.")

Voice-Over: Aren't they having fun? They're sure that they've been good and will soon be given the special gift they've been waiting for—the Messiah!

(Children stop racing around and all sit excitedly in a semicircle DSC.)

Child 1: I'm sure it's almost Messiah time!

Child 2: Yeah. All the signs are right.

Child 3: Good old God. He'll send the gift at the best time—like a big surprise!

Child 4: I always wanted a Messiah action figure.

Child 5: I can hardly wait!

Child 1: I've thought of some great games I want to play with our Messiah.

Child 2: I heard the Messiah will look like King David. He's sure to be handsome—more handsome than [name of a current movie or sports hunk that everyone will recognize].

Child 3: And he has all these features and functions. Like he comes with a full "Destroy the Romans" kit. *(Whoops and makes explosion sound effects the way little boys do when they play war.)*

Child 4: And a "Punish All Gentiles" action. *(Demonstrates fierce karate chops.)*

Child 5: *(Speaking quickly, but not too quickly)* And a "Reinstate Israel as a World Empire Like in the Golden Age of David and Solomon" *(gasps for breath)* function.

Child 1: And he has a throne.

Child 2: And a palace.

Child 3: And a fully restored temple with golden pomegranates on the doors.

Child 4: And he'll be invincible!

Child 5: And we'll all be princes and princesses in his new kingdom!

All: Yea!

John: *(Leaps onstage dramatically from SR.)* Hey, kids! Guess what!

(Children suddenly stop their celebrating and look somewhat confused.)

Child 1: *(In awe)* Wow!

Child 2: Check out the bright, penetrating eyes!

Child 3: And the staff and leather belt.

Child 4: And the locust and honey stains.

Child 5: Could he be…?

All: *(With sudden inspiration)* The Messiah!

John: Hold it! Hold it! I'm not the Messiah.

Child 1: *(Wisely)* I thought the outfit looked a bit Elijah-ish.

All: *(With another sudden-inspiration gasp)* Elijah!

Child 1: It's Elijah! He's back!

Child 2: You know what that means?

All: Messiah time. Yea!

John: I am neither the Messiah nor Elijah. I am John, and I am here to tell you that…the Messiah is coming.

All: Yea! *(Children leap up and dance around with joy.)*

Child 3: And he's bringing the kingdom of God?

John: Yes. So make straight his paths. Flatten the hills, and fill in the valleys.

(Children grab garden rakes and shovels and run around working.)

John: And get everything ready.

(Children grab feather dusters and rush around dusting and straightening things, whether the things are relevant to the plot or not.)

John: Now we must all wash our hands before we receive presents so we aren't dirty anymore. *(Children nod in agreement.)* Come on, into the river, and get washed so you're all ready. *(John leads children across to SR and ceremonially "dunks" each one.)* I wash you with water, but the Messiah will wash you with the Holy Spirit and with fire.

(Children express great excitement. John suddenly pauses and points across to SL dramatically. They all follow his gaze.)

John: And there he is!

(Jesus steps quietly out from SL and stands facing them. Children gasp.)

John: And now my job is done. I must decrease as he increases.

(John quietly steps backward off SR, leaving the Children with Jesus. Jesus walks to DSC, raises his hand in greeting to the Children, and then turns toward the audience, freezing in position. Children excitedly rush over and "surround" him in a semicircle, checking him out.)

Child 1: *(Quietly aside to Child 2)* He's not as big as I thought he'd be.

Child 2: Or as loud.

Child 3: Maybe he's one of those martial-arts experts. He's not all that big, but he's really dangerous.

Child 4: *(Searching around Jesus)* Where's the "Destroy the Romans" button?

Child 5: *(Also searching)* And the "Punish All Gentiles" control?

Child 1: *(With sudden inspiration)* Hey! I know! It's automatic. We don't do anything. It just happens, and we wait and then follow!

Child 2: OK, stand back. Give him room, and we'll see what he does.

Child 3: And be ready. When he calls for war, we wipe out the Romans!

Child 4: *(With Shakespearean grandeur)* Cry havoc, and release the pigs of war.

Child 5: *(Disdainfully)* It's *dogs* of war. Pigs are unclean.

Child 4: *(Ignoring comment)* Oh, look. He's moving. He's going to speak!

Jesus: If any of you want to follow, you must turn from your selfish ways, take up your cross, and follow me. *(He freezes in position.)*

(There is a stunned silence among the Children.)

Child 1: Cross?

Child 2: Must mean "sword." You know, the hand-guard piece looks like a cross.

(Children take some comfort in this but react doubtfully to Jesus' next statement.)

Jesus: Unless you change and become like little children, you will never get into the kingdom of heaven. *(Freezes in position.)*

Child 3: Little children? We're much too big for that!

Child 4: Um…*(Hopefully)* It's probably symbolic.

Child 5: *(With increasing doubt)* Yeah, but of what?

Jesus: Love your enemies! Do good to those who hate you. *(Freezes in position.)*

Child 1: Love your enemies?

Child 2: *(Sounding disgusted)* What's that supposed to mean?!

Child 3: (Searching at Jesus' back or side) This must be just a demonstration mode. Maybe I can find the "Destroy the Romans" switch here.

Child 4: (Helping) It must be here somewhere. I can't even find a control panel. Maybe we should call [name of local computer-game fanatic].

Child 5: (Exasperated) Well, how are we supposed to get him to do stuff without a control panel. (Pokes his finger too hard.) Ow! Twisted my finger!

Jesus: (Without any fuss, turns to Child 5 and touches the finger.) Here, be healed.

Child 5: (With hardly a pause and without noticing) Thanks. (Searching again) Now what about the "Punish All Gentiles" action? You know… (Demonstrates karate chops.)

Child 1: Try moving his arm for him. Maybe it'll kick in.

(Child 2 grabs Jesus' arm and moves it up and down in a karate action, but Jesus speaks as she does it and the movements tie in with the actual words.)

Jesus: Those who use the sword will die by the sword. (Freezes.)

Child 2: There's something wrong. He must be shorting out.

Jesus: Come to me, all of you who are weary and carry heavy burdens, and I will give you rest. Take my yoke upon you. My yoke is easy to bear, and the burden I give you is light.

Child 3: (Giving up in disgust) This is no good! What sort of Messiah present is this? He won't do anything we want!

Child 4: Hope he's still under warranty.

Child 5: (In desperation, he dives in to see if he can find any switch at all.) I'll just try this last…(He is cut off by the next words.)

Jesus: The Messiah must die!

(Children freeze and stare, horrified and silent.)

Jesus: I will go to Jerusalem, and there I will be handed over to the chief priests and scribes. They will kill me, but I will rise after three days.

(The words of the last sentence are muffled by panic-stricken cries from Child 1.)

Child 1: (Yelling) No! No, no, no! This can't be happening!

(Jesus turns toward SR and starts slowly and deliberately to walk off.)

Child 2: (Screaming) Look out! He's heading for Jerusalem. He's going to self-destruct!

Child 3: (In a frenzy) Someone do something!

Child 4: (Rushing in front of Jesus to block him) Hey, you can't die! You're the Messiah. You have to conquer and rule and have thrones and palaces and all that stuff!

Jesus: Get behind me, Satan. You are seeing things from a human point of view, not from God's. (Firmly moves Child 4 aside and walks slowly toward SR.)

(Child 4 is obviously stunned and melts into the background, quieter and more thoughtful than before.)

Child 5: (Furiously) Just what is that supposed to mean!

(Jesus is gone. CD track 1 should slowly get louder offstage.)

Child 1: (Deflated) He's gone.

(Children walk across to SR where Jesus went and stare offstage. Child 4 hangs back dejectedly. Crowd noise becomes more insistent.)

Child 2: Look at that. They got him. He didn't even put up a fight!

(Sound of nails being driven into wood from offstage.)

Child 3: Aw, yuck! Call that a Messiah?

Child 5: Hey, let's see if God will save him.

Child 1: (Calling out) Why don't you call Elijah to see if he'll help you?

Child 2: He's dead.

(The action is obviously over. Crowd noise has faded away. The Children wander back toward SL. Child 4 stops DSC and flops down as the rest go to SL.)

Child 3: Well, that was the biggest letdown!

Child 4: Some present!

Child 5: Yeah, just goes to show that presents aren't always what you expect.

(Children exit SL leaving Child 4 sitting alone DSC. Jesus walks on from SR, sees Child 4 DSC, and walks over to her.)

Jesus: Still here?

Child 4: (Not looking up) Yeah.

Jesus: Where are the rest of the children?

Child 4: They left after the Messiah figure broke. (Looks up and gasps.) What are you doing here? What...but...(Stops, at a loss for words.)

Jesus: (Simply, with no fuss) I'm back.

Child 4: (Struggling) But you broke. They broke you. You weren't...(Leaping to her feet with sudden anger) Why didn't you set up a kingdom?

Jesus: (Simply) I did. It's here. I'm it.

Child 4: (Searching for what to say and how to say it) But you can't be the Messiah! You didn't *do* anything. You didn't *conquer* anything... did you?

Jesus: Did they kill me?

Child 4: Yes.

Jesus: Am I back?

Child 4: (Still not understanding where this is leading) Yes.

Jesus: Well, I conquered death, didn't I?

(Child 4 pauses and then stares at Jesus as he continues. Jesus takes the opportune moment to strike while the iron is hot.)

Jesus: It's an entirely different *kind* of kingdom. And it has started, and it's ready to grow. It's alive. It's kind, too, and it helps and heals people. I need helpers. Will you be in it?

Child 4: (Drops her eyes, assimilating the new concept. She slowly looks up at him again and responds hesitantly but with a note of hope.) You have a nice smile.

Jesus: Thanks.

Child 4: I didn't imagine the Messiah would smile like that. (Stronger) You're a different sort of Messiah.

Jesus: S'pose so.

Child 4: (Taking the plunge) OK. I'm in. We'll tell everyone that the kingdom of God is here, that it's different from what everyone expected, and that you're the Messiah who can't die!

(They link arms and start to march off SL. Child 4 suddenly pauses.)

Child 4: Hey, if you can't die, that means you *are* invincible.

(Jesus smiles.)

Child 4: That's the sort of Messiah I wanted. Hey, you must be in God mode!

Jesus: Permanent God mode.

Child 4: (With an excited, clenched-fist gesture) Yes!

(They link arms again and, happy as a team, march off. Curtain.)

Strain Your Brain, and Stretch Your Faith

Do as many of these activities as time allows.

1. Ask:

> • **What does this skit tell us about human nature and God's nature?**

2. Have the group think of superheroes from comics or movies. List characteristics—their origins, personalities, powers, and specific weaknesses—on a white board.

Then have participants think of strengths and weaknesses of the superhero expected by people of the first century. List these on the white board. Ask:

> • **How do people's pictures of superheroes compare with God's picture of a superhero?**

3. Have participants draw a quick sketch of what they think people of the first century expected the Messiah to look like.

4. Have the group form three smaller groups. A group can be one student. Have each group take two of the following Scripture passages and discuss how they contrast with a superhero stereotype. Allow about 10 minutes for the reading and discussion, and then ask for volunteers to share insights from the discussions.

Matthew 11:1-5   Matthew 18:1-4
Mark 8:31-37   Mark 10:32-34
Luke 6:27-28   Luke 14:27

5. Have participants each find a partner and choose a few of the following Scripture passages. The pair should read the verses and then list the "superhero" power that Jesus demonstrated in each.

Matthew 14:22-32   Matthew 26:62-64
Matthew 28:5-9   Mark 2:1-12
Mark 4:35-41   Mark 6:34-44
Luke 8:26-39   John 2:13-19

6. Bring the group back together and ask:

> • **Why is Jesus the ultimate superhero?**

7. Ask participants to think of people they know whose lives demonstrate Jesus' teaching. List characteristics of these people on the white board. Encourage everyone to choose one characteristic he or she will commit to working on this week.

Lord Jesus, you are our Savior. You are more powerful than any superhero we could think up or imagine. Everything you did for us, you did for free and without waiting for us to deserve it. Thank you for your courage and wonderful love. Give us the faith to follow you and to hold on to the hope that you give us. Amen.

Jonah

And the Moral of the Story Is...
God's purpose, obedience, responsibility

Program Blurb:

We all know that God works in mysterious ways. We also know that he taught Jonah a lesson via the fish-tummy episode. But God sometimes teaches two lessons at once. So who else might have been involved?

What God Says: Jonah 1–3

Handy Info:

The people of Jonah's time would have enjoyed the humorous way God handled the reluctant Jonah. The image of a person being spewed onto the shore by a fish is far from dignified.

But why didn't Jonah want to do the right thing in the first place? Well, the Assyrians, the people who lived in Nineveh, had some interesting habits—executing entire communities by skinning people alive and then nailing the skins to the city wall, for example. No wonder Jonah baulked at the idea of going to Nineveh to tell people they would be punished.

If the group does not already know the story of Jonah, tell the story and discuss this background information before the group reads the script.

Props and Wardrobe:

You'll need a box of matches, a bucket with sand in the bottom, a bucket nearly full of water, and two giant "antacid tablets." These tablets can be two white pillows or two large pieces of Styrofoam. You'll also need a biblical robe for Jonah. The actors doing the parts of God and the Whale stand offstage, so they don't need costumes.

Stage Manager's Clipboard:

You'll need a stage with wings or screens to hide actors.

When Jonah needs to appear wet, the actor can tiptoe to the bucket of water set just offstage, dip his head in it, and go back onstage with water dripping down his robe. Jonah should be sure to keep his hands dry so he can light the matches.

Keep the stage and the room dark throughout the skit. Matches lit by Jonah will provide the only illumination.

Cast List: **Jonah:** totally bewildered

Whale: stuffy and dignified but suffering indignities

God: a "God-like" voice, reverberating or with some quality that will make it obvious that the voice is God's

Cue: The voices of Jonah, God, and the Whale need to be very different.

Cue: While the background sound effects are on the CD, you can no doubt find youth-group members who are good at making really disgusting belches and digestive sounds. Every youth group includes a couple! Have them contribute sound effects at appropriate times, but don't let them get carried away or distract from the action.

Cue: Place the bucket of sand where Jonah can reach it easily with burned-out matches—without tripping over it.

Set the CD to track 2, which will provide a continuous six-minute soundtrack of disgusting digestive noises. Start the CD at the beginning of the skit, and adjust the volume up or down as you wish.

Jonah

(The skit opens with sound effects of digestive gurgles on the CD, track 2.)

Whale: Ooh. Oh. *(Belches.)* Oh. *(Groans.)* I think I ate something weird.

Jonah: *(Onstage but not visible)* Oh, this is disgusting! How do I get into these situations! Yuck. What's that floating past? Can't see a thing.

Whale: *(Groaning)* I haven't felt this bad in ages. *(Belches.)*

Jonah: Oh, this is the pits! It stinks, too. Slime everywhere and all over me! Let's see if I can get one of these going. *(Makes scratching sounds as if trying to light a match.)* No, it's too wet. Try another one. *(Makes more scratching sounds.)* No, it's wet, too. They're supposed to be waterproof! "Ideal for camping, boating, and picnics," the ad said! *(Makes more scratching sounds.)*

Whale: *(Emits a long gurgling belch.)* Yuck. I could feel the bones in that. This is awful.

Jonah: Right, let's see if this one will help. *(Lights a match that reveals him dimly.)* Great! Only I would end up in a dump like this. *(Pauses.)* And what's that groaning noise! *(Looks to one side.)* No, no way out there. Yuck. Bits of dead stuff everywhere. *(Blows out the match as if it burned his finger and drops it in the bucket of sand.)*

Whale: Ooh. I think it's getting worse. A touch of heartburn, too. Oh, I haven't felt this bad since I ate that fishing net. It wasn't my fault. It *looked* like a big wad of noodles. That's the worst thing about being shortsighted and impulsive.

Jonah: *(Strikes another match.)* Why do these things happen to me? Just because I didn't want to go preach in Nineveh. Ridiculous idea to start with. I mean, they wouldn't have listened anyway. They'd skin me alive! They do things like that in Nineveh, you know. *(Starts to walk SR.)* What's over here? *(Blows out match as if it's burning his fingers.)* Ouch!

Whale: Oh, dear! The feeling is moving around. Feels like it's going to and fro! I think I'll try a good dose of antacid pills. *(Gulps loudly.)*

Jonah: *(Strikes a match as two huge white "pills" fly in from SR and hit him.)* Giant pills! Two of them! *(Inspects them.)* I wonder if the Commandments are written on them. *(Blows out match as if it's burning his fingers.)* What else can happen?

Whale: I think I need a good drink of water, too.

(Sound effects of a huge gulp followed by rushing of water, perhaps someone swishing water next to a microphone.)

Jonah: *(Screams. Quickly dips his head in the water and lights a match.)* OK. This is the end! *(Looks around in disgust.)* Seaweed! Digestive juices! Dead prawns! I'm sick and tired of it all! I want out! *(Stomps around, yelling about wanting to get out and then fades his volume down.)*

Whale: Oh, oh, oh! Cramps. Throbbing pain! It's all too much!

Jonah: OK, God. I admit it. It's my fault. I ran away from you. I tried to get out of the task you had for me. I'm sorry!

God: Are you sure?

Jonah: Yes! I promise I won't do it again. I'll start preaching. Just get me out!

Whale: Ooh. That's the limit. All right, God. I admit it. It's my fault. I've been overeating. Wolfing down everything I see. I'm sorry.

God: Are you sure?

Whale: Yes, yes. I'll diet. From now on, it's krill only! Just get me better!

God: Very well.

(Gurgling sounds fade.)

Whale: Oh. Oh…oh, something's happening. I feel weird.

Jonah: Oh. Oh…oh, something's happening. Something feels weird.

(Jonah screams a long drawn-out scream. Sound effects people might make a spewing sound and then a splat.)

Both: *Thank you, God!*

God: *(Chuckling slightly and still very close at hand)* Good. Two jobs done at once.

(Curtain.)

Strain Your Brain, and Stretch Your Faith

Do as many of the following activities as time allows. Make pencils and paper available.

1. Have participants form small groups of three or four. Ask groups to list examples of things Christians are "supposed to do" so they do the will of God in their lives and communities. For example, how should they show Jesus' love in their communities? Then ask groups to make the lists personal by listing what they are willing to do in their own lives and in communities.

2. Bring the group together for this discussion. Ask:

- **What do you find is hardest to do for God? What excuses have you offered for not doing the hard thing?**

- **When have you tried to avoid doing what God wanted you to do?**

- **What distractions and excuses do you and others use to avoid tackling these tasks?**

- **What techniques, such as praying or reading the Bible, do you use to combat the distractions and excuses?**

3. Encourage participants to choose one task from the list of things God wants them to tackle and commit to following through on it this week.

Lord, we can be so weak and distractible when it comes to performing your will and doing the jobs you want us to do. Give us the strength to tackle the tasks, to fight the good fight, and to share your love every day of our lives. Amen.

THE Premeditated Prodigal
And the Moral of the Story Is...
God's forgiveness, God's justice, grace, human nature, relationship with God

Program Blurb:
One character in the story of the prodigal son knows it too well. And he plans to use that knowledge to his own benefit, banking, of course, on dear old dad and his endless capacity to forgive.

What God Says:
Luke 15:11-32

Handy Info:

We are often told that God is a loving and forgiving God, but we rarely think about God's limits. Jesus made it clear that there are points beyond which God is not prepared to go. The parables of the tenant farmers (Matthew 21:33-46), the great feast (Matthew 22:1-14), and the bridesmaids (Matthew 25:1-13) all suggest a limit to God's patience. If we're going to try to manipulate things, counting on a God who will accept us and welcome us back *no matter what*, we may be treading on dangerous ground. God is not a slot machine, nor is he programmed by us.

Before the group reads the drama, have people read and discuss the parable of the prodigal son (Luke 15:11-32) and do the first activity in "Strain Your Brain, and Stretch Your Faith."

Props and Wardrobe:
You'll need trays, drinks, clothes, food, streamers, and so on for the partygoers, as well as an armful of clothes to show to the Son. The Taxi Driver can simply be a person walking and miming use of a steering wheel. (Using real cars should be avoided.)

You can mix and match modern and biblical costumes and props as much as you wish. Use Bible-times robes for the Narrator, the Father, and the Stranger—and for the Son, if you wish, although modern, trendy clothes might be better for him. Partygoers should be modern.

Stage Manager's Clipboard:
A stage with screens or wings for unseen entries and exits would be helpful. However, the skit can also be done in an outdoor setting.

Cast List:

Son: young, trendy, full of himself, and confident that he has the whole scene totally worked out

Other Son: obviously not happy with his brother

Father: wise old man with a touch of humor

Partygoers: any number of assorted waiters, would-be girlfriends, and phony buddies who appear and disappear based on the Son's money

Girl: the only partygoer who shows any real friendship

Taxi Driver: mimes use of a steering wheel

Stranger: a strong presence although he has only one line

Cue: The "party" needs to appear and disappear suddenly and completely.

Cue: The script includes three alternate endings to add breadth to the discussion. Remind youth that the story is an allegory and highly symbolic. Every allegory has its limits, and the features of the story are not to be taken literally. For example, in two endings, the father has died, although God doesn't die, of course. However, in these endings, the father symbolizes the limit of God's forgiveness.

Set the CD to track 3, which provides sounds of a happy party crowd for background. Add up-tempo party music using the venue's sound system, or have someone at the party carry a portable CD player.

TRACK: 3

THE Premeditated Prodigal

(The curtain opens on an empty stage. As the Narrator speaks and the characters appear, they should suggest a stock "narrator drama.")

Narrator: Once there was a man who had two sons. *(Two sons and Father appear and stand DSC.)* They worked the family farm together. *(Father and Sons spread out. Sons mime farm work while the Father patrols.)* The older brother was a reliable worker. *(Father pats Other Son on the back as he passes.)* But the younger brother was dissatisfied. *(Younger brother aims a kick at the ground.)* He felt he wanted to be free, to get away from his father and older brother, and to make his own way in the world. So he said to his father…

Son: *(Interrupting Narrator)* OK, OK. I don't need the prompts. *(Moves DSC and addresses audience.)* I've heard the plot of this one before. *(Recites in a bored, singsong manner)* I go out, have a blast, and then come back and get forgiven *(with sudden enthusiasm)* and start it all again. Hey, it's a bonus.

(Indicates his brother.) Big brother here stays and works. Daddy waits and watches at the gate, fretting and worrying. I party on and repent when it's all spent. What a system! *(Thinks.)*

Now, I have to make it look innocent and spontaneous. *(Approaches Father and falls dramatically on his knees.)* Father, give me the portion of goods that falleth to me.

Father: What? Oh, you mean you want your share now before I kick the bucket.

Son: *(Standing)* Um, yeah. I s'pose that's one way of putting it.

(Father goes sadly to USC and turns away from the audience as if he is getting the cash from a safe.)

Narrator: The father was grieved at his son's request, but…

Son: *(Interrupting dismissively and speaking to the audience)* Yeah, yeah. So he's grieved. He'll get over it. I gotta party. And I come back to get forgiven.

Father: *(Returns with money.)* You sure you want to do this, son? It's a bad…

Son: Yeah, yeah. I'll be careful. *(Snatches the dough.)* Gimme. I know what I'm doing. *(In a stage whisper to audience)* Oh, boy, do I ever know.

Narrator: So, he bade farewell to his father *(Father grabs Son in a tearful bear hug)* and his brother. *(Son saunters past Other Son with a wave of his hand.)* And he journeyed to a far-off land.

(Son walks in circles DSC as Father and Other Son move offstage waving.)

Narrator: He journeyed and journeyed…

Son: Er, can we not make it too far? On account of I want to get quite heavily into the partying, and jetlag tends to cramp my style.

Narrator: At last he arrived in the far-off land, and there he…

Son: Right, thanks a lot. I'll just turn you off now. *(He mimes turning a dial in the air.)* This is where I take it. *(Stops walking DSC.)* Now, let's see. *(Checking off on his fingers)* Far-off land. Yes. Son. Yes. Money. Yes. Now I believe the wording is "and there he wasted all his money in wild living." Oh, yes. Wild living. (Aside) Also translated "loose living," "riotous living," and "disgusting living." (That last one was my own translation.) Oh, man. This is my scene. *(Building up)* OK, guys. Riotous living. *Let's riot!*

(Play CD track 3 and party music. As if from nowhere, Partygoers converge. Son stands DSC, lapping it all up. Merchants bring him clothes to try on. Waiters serve drinks. People dance and congratulate Son. Sound effects fade. Son steps to extreme DSC or even into the audience.)

Son: Oh, man! The years pass. Time flies when you're having fun. I just wish it could go on forever. However, let's check. *(Checks his wallet.)* I think about now things should be running a bit short. Yes, down to the last few dollars.

(To audience) Now all these "friends" will desert me, but that's OK. Watch this. *(He steps back to DSC and, still facing the audience, calls)* Hey, guys. I'm a bit short here. Anyone loan me a 50?

(Instant silence. After three seconds of silence and totally in unison, everyone clears the room until only the Son and Girl USR are left.)

Son: *(Still in the same spot and speaking to audience.)* See? What did I tell you? Do I have this plot organized, or do I?

Girl: *(Hesitantly comes DSC just to SR of Son.)* If you need a little help…

Son: *(Starts violently)* Agh! Who are you? What are you doing here?

Girl: *(Uncertainly)* Well, I felt bad the way they all walked out on you. I could lend you some money if you really need some.

Son: *(Exasperated that her unexpected kindness might be a glitch in his plan)* Um, no. No, no, no. You're… er…you're not supposed to be here.

(Girl looks stunned.)

Son: Look, party's over, OK? *(Starts to escort her off SR.)* You run off home. I gotta get back to the farm and get forgiven so I can start the whole process again. Dad'll forgive me forever. You'll only complicate matters. *(Pushes her off SR and calls after her.)* I'll be back again in a few years. More parties then, OK?

(Returns to DSC dusting his hands and muttering.) Now for the next step. This is the bit where I'm supposed to be poor and hungry and eating pig swill. Gross. You can forget that idea. Now to get a taxi home. *(Calls.)* Taxi.

(Taxi Driver "drives" on. Son climbs in.)

Son: Home, please. You know, the farm in the far country.

(Taxi Driver looks blank.)

Son: You know, the house…with, er, walls…and a roof.

(Taxi Driver nods with sudden understanding as taxi and Son drive.)

Son: Now I'm supposed to look ragged, haggard, and hungry. *(Pulls off his trendy jacket and slings it offstage as they drive.)*

Oh, yeah. Daddykins is supposed to see me coming from far off. *(Calls to Taxi Driver.)* Stop here, thanks.

(Taxi Driver stops SL. Son mimes climbing out and paying Taxi Driver, who drives off SL.)

Son: Now I need to look the part. *(Messes his hair up, pulls his shirt out, slouches, and generally makes himself look ragged.)* And what is it I have to say? Oh, yeah. Sound sorrowful…Father, I have sinned and am no more worthy to be called your son. *(Fakes some tears.)* Let me be a servant in your house.

And it's at that point that he interrupts and calls for the robe and the ring and kills the fatted calf and there's yet *another* party. *(Rubs his hands.)* OK. I'm hungry. Let's do it! *(Walks toward SR, talking as he goes.)* Well, there it is. Now, look sorrowful. Sure is quiet around here. Where's the reception committee? Hey, he must be still inside.

Tsk, tsk, Dad. You're slipping. *(Wagging his finger)* You're supposed to be at the front gate looking for your long lost son. *(By now he is at SR and stops.)* Hmm.

(Son knocks at a door if there is one. If there is no door, Son can mime knocking at an imaginary door as someone offstage makes knocking sounds. Son then faces away and cleans his fingernails. Stranger opens the door, or mimes opening the door, and clears his throat.)

Son: *(Speaking as he turns to Stranger)* Father, I have sinned…Hey, sorry, man. I thought you were someone else. I'm looking for Dad. *(Stranger stares blankly.)* You know, Dad, the old man who owns the farm.

Stranger: You mean the guy before me.

Son: *(Pauses.)* Before you?

Stranger: *(Brutally frank and brief)* He died a year ago. One of his sons ran off, and he never got over it. The older brother sold the farm and moved out.

(Instant blackout. If you can't do a blackout, the Stranger can slam the door as the Son freezes for three seconds and then exits. If there is no door, Son and Stranger should both freeze and then exit.)

ALTERNATE ENDING 1:

Stranger: You mean the guy before me.

Son: *(Blankly)* Before you?

Stranger: The farm's mine now. One of the sons ran off, and the old man waited for years and then finally gave up. He and the other brother sold the farm and moved out. Don't know where.

(Instant blackout. If you can't do a blackout, the Stranger can slam the door as the Son freezes for three seconds and then exits.)

ALTERNATE ENDING 2:

Son: *(Son reaches SL and stops.)* Hmm. *(Son knocks at a door. The person who steps out is his big brother.)* Father, I have sinned and…Hey, bro. *(With confidence)* How you doin', man? Wassup? Hey, where's the old dude? *(Dramatically)* Tell him his son who was lost is now found. He was dead and is now alive.

Other Son: *(Completely blank)* Dad died last year. I'm in charge here now.

(Instant blackout. If you can't do a blackout, both actors freeze for three seconds and then exit.)

Strain Your Brain, and Stretch Your Faith

Do as many of the activities as time allows.

1. Have participants form small groups and choose two or three of the following Scripture passages. (It's OK if more than one group reads the same passage, but be sure all passages are read.) Ask groups to read the verses and then discuss what each passage says about God, about us, about God's justice, and about our responsibilities. Allow time for discussion, and then ask volunteers to share insights about each passage from their groups.

Matthew 18:21-25	Matthew 21:33-46
Matthew 22:1-14	Matthew 24:31-46
Matthew 25:1-13	Mark 3:28-29

2. Have the small groups discuss the point of the skit, choose one ending, and prepare to convince the other groups that it was most effective in making the point. Allow time for discussion, and then have each group present its case.

3. Bring the group back together. Ask:

- **In what way does the prodigal son in this version presume upon the patience and forgiveness of God?**

- **Think of times you have presumed upon God's patience. How might you risk doing what this premeditated prodigal did?**

4. Have participants return to their small groups or form new ones. Have each group write another scene for the skit. Suggest that groups think about these questions:

- **What would the premeditated prodigal son do? Where would he go?**

- **What other characters could be introduced into the scene?**

- **How might repentance and forgiveness be featured?**

If time permits, groups might present their endings.

PRAY

Lord Jesus, thank you for living, dying, and rising again. Thank you for paying the price for our sins. Let us never take for granted what you did or how you suffered for us. Let us always treasure your gift as the wonderful gift it is and work to be the best we can to show our gratitude. Amen.

Zacchaeus

And the Moral of the Story Is...

faith, faith sharing, traditions

Program Blurb:

The Jericho City Council plans to cut down an old tree and put in a modern, landscaped park because "progress can't be stopped." However, workers encounter a protester who feels very attached to the tree. The tree helped the protester find deep meaning, and he believes it could be relevant for others, too.

What God Says:

Exodus 13:19; Luke 19:1-9; 1 Timothy 3:16; 2 Timothy 2:11-13

Handy Info:

Developing sensitivity to the experiences and faith of other Christians is an essential part of growing into Christian maturity and one that's particularly pertinent to teenagers. Since the 1960s, there has been a move to modernize the church, to throw out the old stuffiness and formality. And some fantastic work has been done in contemporary Christian music, informal ways of worship, and modern translations of the Bible.

However, we mustn't confuse making Christianity accessible with just making it trendy. In a quest to be open-minded and modern, we can actually become more narrow-minded than ever. People of all ages can receive inspiration and encouragement from aspects of traditional worship, music, and ritual. Not all traditional things are still useful, but some are. Not all new things are worthy, but some are. We have to be careful to tie the best time-honored elements with the energy and accessibility of the best new things.

At the end of the "Strain Your Brain, and Stretch Your Faith" section is an activity that might lead young participants to an emotional discovery that could change their attitudes toward the faith of others, as well as their own faith. You may want to do the optional activity in a second session after the group has had a chance to discuss themes raised by the skit.

Props and Wardrobe:

You'll need axes, saws, and some rolled sheets of paper (for builders' plans). Actors can indicate the presence of the tree with their actions. The three Workers can wear overalls, jeans, and checked shirts, or other work clothes. Zacchaeus should wear a Bible-times robe.

Cast List: **Zacchaeus:** really remembers that special day

Workers 1, 2, and 3: good-hearted, practical people with a job to do, but open-minded enough to be swayed by a good argument

Cue: If possible, choose a "Zacchaeus" who is significantly shorter than the Workers.

Stage Manager's Clipboard: This skit is a nice, easy one that can be done indoors or out.

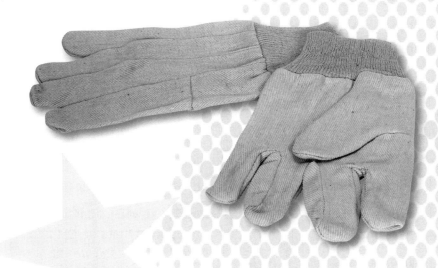

Zacchaeus

(Stage is empty. Worker 1 enters from SR and stops DSC. Unrolls plans, looks around, and looks up as if at a tree.)

Worker 1: All right, this is the one.

(Workers 2 and 3 enter with axes and saws and stop DSC.)

Worker 2: *(Gesturing throughout)* Now, we have to widen here, so we'll take this one *(indicating tree)* out. We'll replant through here. We'll put the new garden there.

Worker 3: And the benches and gazebo go right here. *(Indicates tree.)*

Worker 1: Right. So we start with this old tree.

(Workers prepare to start cutting.)

Zacchaeus: *(Offstage)* Hey! Wait! *(He hurries onstage.)* What are you doing?

Worker 1: We're taking out this old tree. It's part of a new development.

Zacchaeus: You don't mean…this tree! You're not going to cut down *this* one!

Worker 2: No need to get all excited. The whole area is going to be replanted. It'll all be environmentally friendly and totally green.

Worker 3: There'll be more plants here than there were before.

Zacchaeus: But if you're replanting, why are you cutting down the tree?

Worker 1: Oh, it's too old. It's too big. We want to get a new look in here.

Zacchaeus: Who's "we"?

Worker 2: There's a Jericho City Council plan here, as you can see. *(Confidently unfolds the sheet.)* Flowerbeds…shrubs…hedge—a whole revamp.

Zacchaeus: So why can't you leave the tree? It's been here for years. It gives shade.

Worker 3: Yeah, we've considered that, but there'll be a new gazebo.

Zacchaeus: But this tree means something! I mean, it's history. Generations of kids have played here. It holds memories. It's part of people's lives.

Worker 1: Yeah, well, there are some people who don't want it to be part of their lives. We've had a few complaints.

Zacchaeus: Well, you're getting another one right now!

Worker 2: *(Negotiating)* Look, buddy, we have to modernize. Things have to change.

Worker 3: These plans will jazz everything up. It'll be bigger, brighter. There's no practical reason to keep this old tree.

Zacchaeus: Yes, there is. For a start, it's a great climbing tree.

(Workers are nonplussed.)

Zacchaeus: Look. *(He points up into the tree.)* It has pathways all through it. You get a foot in there and swing up to that branch. Then you can reach that one and go up there. You can get right to the top. You can see for miles.

Worker 3: *(Looking up)* Can't see it myself.

Worker 1: Oh, yeah. I can. *(Pointing)* You can swing from that one to there and use it for a rest seat on the way up.

Zacchaeus: That's it. See, once you really look at it, you can see what I mean. You just need someone to explain it. Then you can get into exploring it yourself.

Worker 2: Yeah, well, maybe. But there's going to be a new steel climbing thing.

Zacchaeus: But this is a natural climbing structure. It teaches kids to explore and think and find other branches.

Worker 3: Hey, how come you know about this tree? You used to climb it?

Zacchaeus: Well…yes. Not so long back.

Worker 1: *You* climbed this tree not long ago?

Zacchaeus: It was the only way to see him.

Worker 2: Who?

Zacchaeus: The Son of God.

Worker 1: You saw the Son of God in the tree?

Zacchaeus: No, I was in the tree; he was on the ground.

Worker 2: *(Amused)* And what had you been smoking?

Zacchaeus: No, I mean it. Listen. Jesus was coming through town. I was a tax collector. I wanted to see him, but there was a huge crowd. I couldn't see over the crowd, so I climbed up this tree, onto that branch there and up to that next one and…

Worker 3: Yeah, yeah, OK. What happened?

Zacchaeus: And he stopped right here. He called me down and came to dinner at my house. Me, a tax collector who'd been ripping people off for years. I was never the same again. I gave back the money I'd stolen. I reoriented my whole life. And it's all because of Jesus Christ and that tree. *(Building steam)* That tree is part of my journey, and it can be part of others' journey, too. *(Determined)* If you chop it down, I might have to do something desperate! *(Sticks his chest out and tries to go chin to chin with the biggest worker.)*

Worker 1: *(Convinced by the validity of the story but now in a bind and still with a job to do)* But we have to redesign. *(Looking at the plans)* We have all this new stuff and a limited time frame. After this we have to remodel [inserts name of popular local character's garden/house/carport/bedroom or whatever is best for a good joke]. It's a big job.

Zacchaeus: You're right. That *is* a big job. *(With sudden inspiration)* Hey, why can't you *include* the tree? *(Takes the plans excitedly.)* Look, landscaping needs different levels, right? Well, make the tree a feature! Complement the flowerbed…contrast the hedge. Put the gazebo next to it, and the two will give better shelter *together*.

Worker 2: *(Considering)* I suppose we could use it as a centerpiece for this section.

Zacchaeus: *(Hands plans back.)* Now you're talking.

Worker 3: We'll have to get approval from the Jericho City Council.

Worker 1: But I think we can make a good argument. Historical, aesthetic, educational, practical use, sentimental attachment, keeping the best of the past for the future… that sort of thing.

Zacchaeus: *(Slapping them on their backs.)* Cool! Hey, thanks for being open-minded! You restore my faith in human nature. *(The Workers start to pack up and are about to move off SR again.)* By the way, when you put in the steel climbing structure, do you think you could put it here so it's close to that large branch up there?

Worker 2: Why?

Zacchaeus: *(Self-consciously)* Well, if I happen to be climbing the tree, just for memory's sake or to show some kids the way up, I could… er…also swing across and try out the new climbing structure. I mean, the new ones are fun, too, you know.

(Zacchaeus links arms with two of the Workers. All march off together. Curtain.)

Strain Your Brain, and Stretch Your Faith

Do as many of the following activities as time allows.

1. Have the groups form small groups of three or four to discuss the following questions. Allow time for discussion after each question, and then ask volunteers to share insights with the group.

   • **What do the tree and the new climbing structure represent? Why does Zacchaeus ask that the new climbing structure be put close to the tree? What point does this make?**

   • **Read 1 Timothy 3:16 and 2 Timothy 2:11-13. These words are actually from hymns and creeds of the early church and would have been sung and recited by the first Christians 2,000 years ago.**

   • **How does reading words sung by the first Christians make you feel?**

   • **Do you feel responsible for preserving their words? Why or why not?**

2. Identify three *well-liked and respected* older Christians or Christian couples, each representing a particular decade or era in the church community's history. Invite these Christians to your youth group meeting.

   To prepare for your guests, have your group think of questions for them. Some questions might be

   • **When did your association with the church begin?**

   • **When did you become a committed Christian?**

   • **What are some of your best memories of life and events in our church community?**

   • **What are some of your personal favorite hymns/prayers/readings/events/traditions that have helped you through specific tough times in your life?**

After participants have listened to the guests, have them ask themselves the same questions. Encourage them to think about things in worship and in their Christian life that they enjoy, grow from, and want to see passed on. After youth group members and guests have shared ideas, follow up with prayer.

PRAY

Lord, thank you for all Christians who have made up your great family and for those of us who are still part of your church on earth. Help us be inclusive in our worship, be open-minded in our approach to others, and value and learn from the faith journey of other Christians. Amen.

How to Speak Christian

And the Moral of the Story Is...
Christian subculture, exclusiveness, faith sharing, relationships

Program Blurb:
This skit is a parody of TV shows that claim to teach people to speak English or some other language through carefully arranged and subtitled "conversations." In this skit, the audience can hear the Christian "language."

What God Says:
Matthew 13:10-17; 1 Corinthians 9:19-22

Handy Info:

Who wouldn't understand us Christians? We're just ordinary people, and we just talk ordinary talk...don't we? Well, yes, usually. But we have to be very careful because there *is* Christian jargon that a newcomer would find hard to deal with. This jargon can be found even in modern praise songs. We think of these songs as inclusive because the beat is modern, but some are language exclusive. Being a Christian means spreading the good news, so it's important that we don't use "in" talk that might alienate people.

Before your group reads the script, have participants spend a few minutes on the first "Strain Your Brain, and Stretch Your Faith" activity. It is very valuable for young Christians to have to verbalize exactly what they are talking about when it comes to their faith and beliefs.

Props and Wardrobe:
No props are needed. That is, the actors do wear clothing of some sort, but it can be modern stuff. You'll also need chairs if the speakers are to be seated.

Stage Manager's Clipboard:

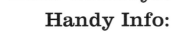

Use the PDF (portable document format) file on the CD to print subtitles for cue cards. Have someone hold up the cue cards at the side of the stage. (Note that one translation subtitle is not in the PDF file—the one for which you insert the name of a well-known youth group or church community person in a humorous context. If you're using cue cards, you'll need to make this one.)

Set the CD to track 4, which provides intro and exit music.

You could also have an offstage Voice-Over say the translation in a clear but bland voice after each line. The conversation can take place anywhere. You could have a living-room setting or just have two people walk across the stage and greet each other.

Cast List: **Person 1 and Person 2:** Both should speak at a very steady pace with somewhat exaggerated expression and very over-the-top facial responses to the other's lines. They should show exaggerated interest in each other, with hugely friendly greetings and very big smiles at the audience at the end.

Voice-Over: very bland and steadily paced

Cue: Ensure Persons 1 and 2 pause between lines to give the audience time to read/assimilate the translation.

Cue: Conversational language changes all the time, and expressions that are cool today will be passé tomorrow. This script is very flexible. Alter the lines to whatever would be considered in for your audience. The main thing is to have the stilted Christian language expressions changed to everyday expressions.

How to Speak Christian

(*Fade in intro music on CD track 4.*)

Voice-Over: Welcome to *How to Speak Christian*: "Lesson 1: Greetings and General Conversation."

(*Fade out intro music. Lights come up on two people on stage or, if no lights, the two can simply enter from opposite sides of the stage and meet DSC. They greet each other with exaggerated waves and facial expressions.*)

Person 1: The peace of the Lord be with you.

(**Translation:** Hi.)

Person 2: And also with you.

(**Translation:** Hi.)

Person 1: How's your spiritual life?

(**Translation:** How ya doin'?)

Person 2: I've been blessed this past week.

(**Translation:** Been fine, thanks.)

Person 1: Hallelujah.

(**Translation:** That's good.)

Person 2: Amen.

(**Translation:** Yeah, that's good.)

Person 1: How has the grace of God been made manifest in your life?

(**Translation:** Wassup?)

Person 2: I've been walking in faith and victory and rejoicing along the way.

(**Translation:** Things are cool.)

Person 1: Amen.

(**Translation:** That's good.)

Person 1: I've been searching the Scriptures and seeking the guidance of the Lord on a personal matter.

(**Translation:** I've been wondering.)

Person 2: Has your stewardship of material blessings been unwise?

(**Translation:** You broke again?)

Person 1: No, I have been given victory over the hunger and thirst of the flesh.

(**Translation:** Today is payday.)

Person 2: God has given me a real burden for you and your level of Sunday-night devotional commitment.

(**Translation:** Are you busy Sunday night?)

Person 1: I'm free of slavery to worldly and temporal things.

(**Translation:** No.)

Person 2: Would you care to fellowship at the community of the faithful wherein I am spiritually nourished?

(**Translation:** Want to come to my church?)

Person 1: At what stage of church growth and development is your Christian family network?

(**Translation:** What's it like?)

Person 2: The Spirit moves in that assembly and the born-again brothers and sisters have a real burden for the extension of the Barnabas ministry of encouragement and acceptance…

(**Translation:** They're friendly people.)

Person 2: and a true sense of the Scripturally humorous aspect of creation.

(**Translation:** [Name of youth group member] comes to the meetings, too.)

Person 1: Into what areas of active worship will I be led?

(**Translation:** What will we do?)

Person 2: We will partake in small-group fellowship.

(**Translation:** We all sit around in little groups…)

Person 2: and share.

(**Translation:** and talk.)

Person 2: Then we come together for a total worship experience seeking his face in prayerful supplication…

(**Translation:** Then we join in the church service…)

Person 2: with psalms, hymns, and spiritual songs.

(**Translation:** and sing.)

Person 1: Contemporary gospel music?

(**Translation:** Christian rock songs?)

Person 2: Amen.

(**Translation:** You know it, man.)

Person 2: With daily miracles, fire, and signs following.

(**Translation:** We all groove on.)

Person 2: Then there is the sacrament of the bread and the fruit of the vine.

(**Translation:** There's a Lord's Supper service tonight.)

Person 2: And after the benediction…

(**Translation:** At the end…)

Person 2: we hold the agape feast…

(**Translation:** we all pig out…)

Person 2: in the youth-group room…

(**Translation:** in the basement…)

Person 2: and share the exultation.

(**Translation:** and party on.)

Person 1: I feel I've been given a word from the Lord to share with you.

(**Translation:** Yeah, I'll come.)

Persons 1 and 2: Amen.

(*Both turn to smile at the audience in that phony "show host" way and freeze as the music fades in and Voice-Over does its final thing. Or both people can exit any side together.*)

Voice-Over: Next week, we look at redemption, justification, and the concept of leaning on God.

(*Music fades. Curtain, exit, or blackout.*)

Strain Your Brain, and Stretch Your Faith

Do as many of the following activities as time allows.

1. Before youth group members read the script, have them spend just a few minutes brainstorming about jargon. Give each person a piece of paper, and ask participants to fold the paper lengthwise to make two columns. (Or make two columns on a white board.)

   Ask participants to think of technical jargon associated with computers, sports, or anything else. Ask them to list the term in one column and the translation in the second column. Then ask them to list "Christian-ese" terms and translations.

   After a very brief brainstorm session, have your group read the script. After the reading, have people look at the lists again to see if the skit prompted any more ideas.

   (The idea is not only to list some more Christian "in" expressions but to actually grapple with explanations and definitions. Suggest *salvation, atonement, faith, forgiveness,* and *grace* if no one suggests these terms. Also suggest that participants think of lyrics to modern praise songs, which can be a goldmine of Christian-ese terminology.)

2. Ask people to think about their lists as they discuss these questions.

   - **How can this sort of language make it hard for non-Christians to understand what is going on?**

   - **What do Matthew 13:10-17 and 1 Corinthians 9:19-22 tell us about how we should share our faith with others?**

   - **We want to be accessible in the way we talk to people about our faith and Christian experience, but we don't want to water down the meaning of what is, after all, a powerful faith relationship with God. How can we ensure that we are understandable but not bland?**

   - **What can we learn from the way Jesus communicated his powerful message and still retained the interest and respect of his listeners?**

Lord, teach us to speak to those around us in ways they will hear and understand. Give us the wisdom to see past words that conceal who people are and even who we are. Give us the determination to know people for who they really are. Give us the courage to spread the good news of your love in ways that will truly speak to the hearts and minds of all we contact. Amen.

Complaints to the Management

And the Moral of the Story Is...
church communities, criticism, gratitude, prayer

Program Blurb:
Some people are habitual complainers for whom nothing is ever good enough. In Australia they're called "whingers" (pronounced win-jas). Well, three whingers decide that church is too boring, so they phone God to complain.

What God Says: Matthew 11:16-19; 1 Corinthians 12:12-20; 2 Corinthians 11:21-29

Handy Info: Too many people both in and out of the church are quick to criticize the church and the people in it. But with a relatively safe target like the church, it is too easy to dish out complaints and yet do nothing to improve what's not perfect. Some people go to church in a "concert" frame of mind—ready to be entertained. Church communities and worship are much more than that. It's we who should be performing for God, not the other way around.

Props and Wardrobe: You'll need a phone onstage. The characters should look sloppy to reflect their attitude.

Stage Manager's Clipboard:

Decide how you want to use the complaint signs. You could tape them up before the skit where the audience can read them. Or Complainers who aren't actually speaking on the phone at that moment might hold them up or attach them to a wall, the curtain, or a tree (if you're performing outdoors).

Before the group reads the script, lead participants in a discussion of questions 1 through 3 in the "Strain Your Brain, and Stretch Your Faith" section.

Cast List: **Complainers 1, 2, and 3:** real whingers (Complainer 2 needs to be male; the others can be any gender.)

Cue: The group can have lots of fun working out the mimed actions for the Complainers to use to illustrate what is being described on the phone. Be careful of actually imitating known people from the congregation, though.

You'll find some fun complaint signs on the CD. Print them out, and use them for visual reinforcement of what the Complainers say.

Complaints to the Management

(Complainers enter from any side and begin to complain as they advance to DSC.)

Complainer 1: Oh, man. Life is getting more boring every day. It's criminal. Everything is just so tedious.

Complainer 2: Like church services at that church of ours.

Complainer 3: Now *that's* boredom!

Complainer 1: Why doesn't God do something about it?

Complainer 2: It's s'posed to be his church, isn't it?

Complainer 3: For real!

Complainer 1: Yeah. If I could reach him, I'd complain.

Complainer 2: Well, why don't you?

Complainer 1: Why don't I what?

Complainer 2: Why don't you talk to God and complain?

Complainer 1: Oh, sure. How am I going to do that?

Complainer 3: Call him.

Complainer 1: Aw, you can't phone God. What are you talking about?

Complainer 2: Of course you can. Give him an earful. What's he there for?

Complainer 1: *(Purposefully advancing toward the phone)* All right, I will. *(Picks up phone and hesitates.)* Hey, I wonder what his number is.

Complainer 2: Try 777.

Complainer 1: Yeah, that should get him. *(Dials furiously. Waits and then indicates that phone is answered.)* Hello, God? Yeah, it's us. We want to complain. *(Pauses.)*

What about? Church services at that church of ours, that's what. I mean, have you ever been in one? Were you there last week?

You were! *(Looks at others.)*

Complainer 3: Lucky we went.

Complainer 1: *(Speaking into phone)* Well, I want to complain about them. *(Pauses.)* What part of them? *(Laughs nonchalantly.)* How long do you have?

(Stops laughing abruptly.) Eternity. Oh, yeah. I forgot. Well...for a start...

(Complainers 2 and 3 wildly signal and begin to mime singing a hymn with doleful faces. From this point on, as the Complainers pass the phone around, the others mime whatever the one on the phone is talking about and display the appropriate complaint sign.)

Complainer 1: Well, for a start there are those doleful hymns, Lord. They're enough to put a sidewalk to sleep. And that organist. He doesn't play the organ; he drives it...like a tractor. If you're lucky, you're singing at the rate of about one word a second by the end of the song.

Complainer 2: *(Snatches the phone.)* Not to mention the sermons. When you visit our church, make sure you wear a sweater 'cause the sermon lasts at least one ice age. And what about the guys who pass the collection bowls? They just about shove them up your nose. Anyone would think you're supposed to put something in it! I have compassion fatigue. It's give, give, give!

Complainer 3: And what about the pews in that place? What are they made of—the rare and extinct concrete-wood tree? It's like trying to sleep on *(catches himself/herself)* I mean, it's like trying to sit on a camel skeleton.

Complainer 1: And speaking of wooden structures, the floorboards in that church are rotting under our feet. I was walking down the aisle the other day, and I hit a rotten patch and went straight down. Thought it was the rapture and I was going the wrong way.

And the organ pipes in that place need a real good cleaning and service. We have possums building nests in the organ pipes! That E pipe is so blocked up that when the organist hit a hard E note the other day, the air pressure built up and the pipe took off and went straight through the roof. It blew up at 900 feet. Now the neighbors think the church is a secret army missile base.

Complainer 3: And what about the lawns? What does the landscaper mow them with? A flamethrower? He probably uses a chainsaw to do the edges. He's probably the same karate expert who arranges the flowers on the altar. Best place for them, too. They're only fit for burnt offerings.

Complainer 1: And what about that awful Christian band that visits us once a month like the plague? Half of them couldn't play the radio, let alone instruments. They're supposed to be "enlivening" the service. They couldn't enliven a bottle of grape juice. I've thrown shoes at alley cats making better noises than they do.

Complainer 2: And that cruddy Christian drama group that gets up in front of the congregation to gratify their egos. Where do they get their scripts—a pharmacy rubbish bin?

Complainer 3: And what about the B-grade Christian dancers who flaunt their bodies in front of everyone?

Complainer 1: I don't know where they get these types. They're the dregs of the universe. We could do better ourselves. *(Others nod in agreement. Complainer 1 pauses.)*

Eh? What? What do you mean, "Why don't you?" *(Complainer 1 suddenly becomes rather tense and nervous.)*

No, no, I don't preach. I'm not getting up there in front of all those people! *(Passes phone to Complainer 2.)*

Complainer 2: No, I don't lead youth group. Not with all those rotten kids! *(Passes phone to Complainer 3.)*

Complainer 3: No, I don't mow the lawns. I can't do that heavy physical work 'cause I have a broken bladder. *(Pauses.)*

What do we do? *(Looks helplessly at the others for assistance. They shrug and stare blankly back.)*

Um…we don't do anything. *(Pauses.)*

Hello. Hello? Hello! *(Turns to others.)* He hung up. Just when we were getting warmed up.

(All three Complainers wander offstage discussing how they were "just having a talk about the church when he suddenly hung up." Curtain or blackout.)

Strain Your Brain, and Stretch Your Faith

After the group has discussed the first three questions, read the script, and discussed the background information, have them discuss as many of the remaining questions as time allows.

- **What are some of the common complaints you hear about church?**

- **What are some of the common complaints you hear about Christians?**

- **What have you complained about?**

- **What can you do about the things you've complained about?**

- **What is the point made in Complainer 3's final words?**

- **What common stereotypes about church and Christians do you see in the media?**

- **How can you help explode these stereotypes?**

- **Read Matthew 11:16-19 and 2 Corinthians 11:21-29. How does it make you feel to know that Jesus and Paul also had to put up with complainers and with their own problems?**

Lord, we offer our praises to you for all we have. Compared to many in the world today and in times past, we have it easy. Forgive us when we complain and gripe about things and yet do nothing constructive about them. Give us the wisdom and the strength to get involved in our own church community, in our youth group, and in our worship services. Help us participate and live our Christian faith in a real way. Amen.

The Youth-Group Two-Step

And the Moral of the Story Is...
church communities, human nature, peer pressure, relationships, youth groups

Program Blurb:
This skit takes a hard-hitting look at the way youth groups can be abused by members who use the group as an ego forum, a fashion show, a social-status vehicle, or a place to maneuver for sympathy.

What God Says: Micah 6:6-8; Luke 10:25-27; Acts 6:1; 1 Corinthians 1:10-13; 3:1-3; 13:4-7; Ephesians 4:14-15

Handy Info: The skit juxtaposes the misuse of youth groups with a positive view of how a group should function. It is also a good vehicle for illustrating that cliques and power plays have always been problems in the church—just as they are in any institution that includes humans. In 1 Corinthians 1:10-13 and 3:1-3, Paul responded to some of the problems the church faced in its earliest days. How might he have reacted to your youth group if he were to visit?

Props and Wardrobe: No props are needed. Costumes should be appropriate for a barn dance.

Stage Manager's Clipboard: You'll need a good-size stage for the "barn dance" effect. The caller's words need to be heard clearly, so make sure people don't stomp their feet too much onstage. The caller should say the **bold** lines to the rhythm of the music. All other lines should be spoken in a normal, conversational way.

Cast List: **Dancers:** any number of high-energy couples

CALLER: someone with a precise sense of rhythm, seen or unseen (If the Caller is offstage, he or she doesn't have to memorize the lines.)

Cue: The skit includes dance steps, but your group may choose to alter the steps or improvise new steps. Some lines—about the saddest tale of woe, for example—lend themselves to dramatic, exaggerated miming. Symbolic dance-style movements might go with other lines.

Use track 5 on the CD for barn-dance music.

TOP 20 SKITS

TRACK: 5

The Youth-Group Two-Step

(Stage is empty at the start.)

CALLER: Ladies and gentlemen, take partners for the Youth-Group Two-Step.

(Dancers run excitedly onstage and line up on opposite sides of the stage, with each dancer across the stage from a partner. Dance music begins.)

CALLER: Bow to your partner, shake hands at the door, bow to the new kid, talk to the new kid, feel uncomfortable with the new kid, and turn back to your partner.

(Dancers skip forward, bow in various directions, and mime talking uncomfortably to an imaginary "new kid.")

CALLER: Now, waltz your partner to and fro; check out who's wearing trendy clothes.

Check out who wants to run the show— when the meeting starts, you'll be in the know.

(Couples waltz madly to and fro, looking over each other's shoulder to check out what everyone else is wearing.)

CALLER: Now, line up in order of status…and maneuver!

(Dancers rush to form a line DSC to USC and begin trying to shoulder their way to the DS front of the line.)

CALLER: Maintain your power in the youth group. Don't let your partner usurp your position.

Now, waltz your partner in and out— and who's on top, there is no doubt.

If social status you would seek, come wearing trendier clothes next week.

(Dancers go back to waltzing around, stopping occasionally to point at their clothes and pose.)

CALLER: Now, all come out for sharing time, and everyone will stand in line.

See who's got the saddest story to tell; see who's sorry, who's not well.

(Dancers form a single line along the DS side of stage, from SL to SR, facing the audience, clap and stomp in time with the music. One by one the dancers stand forward from the DSR end of the line and, with flamboyant gestures, "tell" their tales, getting worse at the end of the line.)

CALLER: Oh, that was a good one. Oh, that one was better. These are better still! Oh, listen to this one…my aunty's uncle's best friend's cat died. That's the best of all! It wins this week!

(The winner bounces around making a victory sign while the other dancers fling their hands in the air in frustrated movements. Couples join and spin.)

CALLER: So spin your partner left and right, more sympathy next Friday night.

This week a trauma will fill your cup; if that doesn't happen, just make one up!

Now it's time for discussion groups. All get into discussion groups. Have your gossip ready—who's going out with whom.

(Dancers form small groups whispering and pointing.)

CALLER: Now, promenade your partner around; discuss and talk with lots of sound.

(Dancers promenade around and around, making exaggerated discussing and talking movements as they go.)

CALLER: Don't let your opinion be put down; now disagree on theological grounds.

(Having suddenly split on the word disagree, couples turn back to do-si-do.)

CALLER: Turn your back on your partner (do-si-do); into an issue let it grow.

Don't talk to your partner (do-si-do); to another youth group you will go.

And schism…split right up…

(Dance partners split and march aggressively to opposite sides of the stage.)

CALLER: And schism again…

(Former partners pass each other center stage as they march across to opposite side of stage again, sticking their tongues out at each other as they go. They end up on opposite sides from their old partners and are now ready to take new ones.)

CALLER: And change partners.

Now backslide. (New couples link arms and slide-walk backward to US.)

All the way now, and backslide some more. And onto another stage.

For weeks you've been on a spiritual low; your cup of life is filled with woe.

It's off to a youth group camp you go. There's sexy hunks and chicks, you know.

(Dancers droop aimlessly around the stage, looking depressed. Then they perk up and march into a revolving circle to symbolize going to camp.)

CALLER: Now repent…

(Dancers jump and turn to march in opposite direction.)

CALLER: You find yourself surrounded by sympathetic and attractive members of the opposite sex. Repenting got so much attention that you do it again. Repent again—it works so well.

Now you go into a spiritual high; you love the world and have a cry.

(Dancers go berserk with happiness, kicking their heels up, dancing, and waving their hands in "praisey" motions.)

CALLER: On Sunday you go home, straight into a spiritual low.

(Dancers go from dancing round to a bent-double, depressed posture.)

CALLER: Go to a weekend retreat, and have a spiritual high. Go home, and have a spiritual low. Go to a seminar. Have a spiritual high. Go home. Have a spiritual low. That's it: up and down like a yo-yo. Spiritual highs and lows all over the place. But it finally hits you how pointless all this is.

(Dancers go through this up/down movement several times.)

CALLER: By now you're getting sick of this; the main point you have obviously missed.

What's youth group about? You think it through. What would Jesus do?

(Dancers pause to adopt a "thinking" posture.)

CALLER: (Confidentially) You get the impression there must be more to being a Christian in a youth group…right?

(Dancers nod in unison. Then with determined faces, the dancers form a circle DSC and join hands to revolve, lifting their hands on the "worship God" cue.)

CALLER: You go…back to youth group to do it right. No power play on Friday night!

You're all in this to help along and worship God in word and song.

You walk together on the road; you help each other bear the load

(Tears are good when tears are real); be there for friends; feel how they feel.

(Dancers march in the circle, patting each other on the back and forming a comforting tableau around a single upset member for the "tears are good" cue.)

CALLER: Discussion groups and sharing time, singing, praying will combine

To make it work like God's design, but only when they're gen-u-ine.

(Dancers can break into tableaus to illustrate each.)

CALLER: So waltz your partner 'round and 'round. A steady faith is what you've found.

(Dancers waltz again happily.)

CALLER: Now, everyone is welcome here; it doesn't matter what they wear.

Bow to your partner. Wave to your corner.

Give your partner a hug. Give your corner a pat.

And out you go to share your faith.

(Dancers give a wild "yeehaw" and dance out in line, throwing their hats in the air or some such festive movement. Curtain.)

Strain Your Brain, and Stretch Your Faith

Do as many of the following activities as time allows.

Have participants form small groups of three or four to discuss the questions. Provide paper and pens. After participants discuss each question in their small groups, ask volunteers to share thoughts with the larger group.

1. Say: **List the mistakes members of the skit's youth group made.** Ask:

   • **What was the attitude behind many of these mistakes?**

   • **What change of attitude would help to solve many of the problems?2.** Say: **Read the following Scripture passages: Acts 6:1; 1 Corinthians 1:10-13; 3:1-3; 13:4-7; and Ephesians 4:14-15.** Ask:

   • **What problems did those Christian communities have?**

   • **What does this show about human nature?**

3. Say: **Read Micah 6:6-8 and Luke 10:25-27. Then list what you think the real goals and priorities should be for a Christian youth group. (They don't have to be in order of importance.)**

4. **Read 1 Corinthians 1:10-13; 5:1-2; and 11:17-22 for a taste of the Apostle Paul's words to a church community with real problems. He set people straight in no uncertain terms. What would Paul write to the youth group in the Two-Step? In your small groups, imagine you're Paul and write to that youth group. Let them have it! (But be careful…What might Paul say to *your* group?)**

Lord Jesus, as we have made you Lord of our lives, help us always keep you as Lord of our youth group. Keep us from selfishness or narrow-mindedness. Help us always keep our focus on you and live for you, following the example you set. Amen.

Honesty

And the Moral of the Story Is...
confession, doubt, faith, prayer, relationship with God, suffering

Program Blurb:
A person begins to pray, beginning just the way he or she has prayed for years. But is it all a mask? What real feelings and fears lurk below the surface?

What God Says: Psalm 70; Matthew 26:36-46; John 6:66-69; 2 Corinthians 11:23b-27

Handy Info: This skit is suitable for linking with readings from the "troubled" psalms or from Ecclesiastes. It is a hard-hitting one that deals with emotions many people feel but are afraid to express. Doubts aren't trendy; nor are questions, failings, or fears. It's too risky to admit doubts and fears, especially in the triumphal, never-fail atmosphere reigning in some congregations.

Yet any Christian who is honest will admit to having doubts. It's part of the human condition. Paul had bad days; so did the prophets. God's people throughout the ages have suffered and been persecuted and often come close to giving up. To say, "Well, they must have lacked faith," is simplistic and damaging. Such statements have led many to misunderstand and discard their Christian faith. Our God is forgiving and understanding, and he knows we struggle to comprehend. He can handle our anger and our doubts.

This drama will elicit a positive and heartfelt response from many participants who feel better knowing there are others who feel the same doubts and fears they often do.

Props and Wardrobe: You'll need a chair. The Person should wear normal clothes.

Stage Manager's Clipboard: You'll need an offstage microphone for the Voices. **Set the CD to track 6** to provide some formal church music for a "churchy" atmosphere.

Cast List: **Person:** knows how to say the "right" type of prayer but inside has a lot of doubts

Voices 1, 2, and 3: the Person's feelings and doubts, which have their own voices at last

Cue: The Person starts off with an "I am here to worship in the correct and holy manner" attitude, so his or her posture and attitude at the start should be fairly formal.

Honesty

(Play track 6 on the CD. Person enters, obviously in "spiritual worship mode," and sits on the chair to pray. The Person can also be already sitting as lights come up or curtain is opened. Music fades.)

Person: Dear Lord, thanks for the week you've given me with its many experiences and opportunities. Thanks for guiding me over the rough patches and for giving me a very real sense of your presence.

Voice 1: *(Groaning)* Oh, brother.

Person: *(Stops and looks around.)* Thanks for giving me a very real sense of…

Voice 2: *(Stronger.)* Oh, brother! *(Person looks around again.)* How can you say that?

Person: *(Mystified.)* Eh?

Voice 3: How can you say that tripe? Your face ought to be red!

Person: *(Standing to look around.)* Who's talking?

Voice 1: Oh, come on. You know.

Person: *(Flopping down into chair)* Oh no, not you.

Voice 2: Oh yes, it's us. Or should I say, "Oh yes, it's you"?

Person: Well, I'm not going to listen to you.

Voice 3: You said that last week and the week before and the year before!

Person: *(Pushing on)* Oh Lord, thanks for giving me a very real sense of…

Voice 1: *(Talking over Person and building to a shout)* Cliché, cliché, cliché! We're still here!

(Person gives up praying in frustration.)

Voice 1: You can't shout us down because we just get louder. You don't really believe half that stuff.

Person: Enough!

Voice 2: You don't know for sure about most of that stuff you just said.

Person: *(Looking nervously around)* I said, "Be quiet." Someone will hear.

Voice 3: *(As loud as before)* As a matter of fact, you're not even sure there is a God. You're afraid you might be just tossing words up at the stars.

Person: *(Self-righteously)* I am not!

Voice 1: You are so! And I know because you're only there on the ceremonial outside. I'm in here, where it all happens.

Person: *(As if quoting the Bible)* Get thee behind me, Satan, oh, thou bringer of doubt.

Voice 2: Oh no. It's not Satan this time. You can't palm the responsibility off to some bad-guy figure. This is yourself talking here. These doubts are yours.

Person: Yeah, well, go away. I'm praying.

Voice 3: You're not. You're mouthing. You're performing. You're only in this church because you feel guilty if you don't go.

Person: What?

Voice 1: You think church is basically boring. You have ever since you were a kid, when you'd sit and wish you could be outside playing. You still feel that way. Like you want to be out there doing something active…*(driving the point home)* doing something "real," as I once heard you think.

Person: Oh, come on. That's not fair. All I meant was…

Voice 2: And speaking of real, why don't you pray a real prayer? Why don't you ask about the rotten week you just had? Experiences and opportunities, ha! Why not ask why everything got messed up in front of your eyes? Even the things you prayed for.

Person: Well, God works in mysterious ways, and we don't know…

Voice 3: Yeah, he works in mysterious ways, all right. First, he tells us in the Bible that if we pray for something, we'll get it. And then, when we do pray, half the time nothing happens. What a big con job!

Person: But it isn't that simple!

Voice 1: Oh, come on. Don't give me all the old copouts. You know the verses yourself. "Ask anything in my name," I think was the wording. And what about "knock and the door shall be opened, ask and you shall receive"? You know them all because you read them yourself at the prayer meeting you went to where you prayed for the farmers who were losing everything because of the drought…*(pushing it)* didn't you?

Person: *(Grudgingly)* Yeah, so what?

Voice 2: Well, how many months ago was that?

Person: *(More grudgingly)* Ten.

Voice 3: And what about the drought? Worse than ever, isn't it? Farmers forced off their properties. Families broken up. *(Pauses.)* Suicides. *(Pauses.)* Well?

Person: *(Desperately searching)* The hardship has brought the community closer together.

Voice 1: Yeah, well, you try telling that to the farmers. You prayed for the drought to end, and it didn't. Just like the famine in Ethiopia [or somewhere topical]. You've been praying about that one for the last five years. And it's still happening. Kids dying like flies. The kids *he's* supposed to care for.

Person: *(Begins to pace uncomfortably, kicking at the floor, trying to deal with all this.)* But that's not just the drought. It's the greed of the politicians and the warlords.

Voice 2: Well, why doesn't he take the politicians and the warlords and close them down?

Person: *(Desperately)* But he weeps for the suffering children. He suffers, too.

Voice 3: Oh, that's a great comfort, isn't it? God in heaven, where everything's lovely, weeps for the suffering children! Look, you're a parent, aren't you? Well, just imagine that you're sitting by a playground watching your kids playing happily when suddenly a group of thugs comes along and starts to beat up your kids. So what do you do? Sit and weep for them? Of course not! Any parent worth their salt wades in and does something.

Person: But God has his wrathful side. He will take vengeance on those who…

Voice 1: But when, friend, *when*? How many more kids have to die? How many more families have to be machine gunned before he does something?

(Pauses. Then with a quiet, threatening note) And it's not just overseas and in the Midwest, is it? It's closer to home, isn't it?

(Person acts uncomfortable, perhaps pacing or sitting hunched over.)

Voice 2: What about Brian Wilson, eh? Killed in his car with his two friends. His father was a minister. Don't tell me no one ever prayed for him. But the tire blew out anyway.

Person: *(Stumbling on, though he or she knows the words sound pathetic)* But his fiancée got out of it. She was such a wonderful witness to the nurses in the hospital.

Voice 3: Well, I suppose she had to be, didn't she. She has to have something to hold on to now that she's a *paraplegic*. All those kids had been prayed about a million times. *(Pauses.)* Just like people prayed for Cathy.

(Person stands stock still, facing away from the audience. There is silence. This is the final blow.)

Voice 2: They did pray for Cathy, didn't they?

Person: *(With undisguised and rising anger)* Yeah!

Voice 3: How many times?

Person: Dozens.

Voice 1: And they claimed healing and wholeness and health…didn't they?

Person: Yeah.

Voice 2: *(Strongly)* And what happened when the pain got too much for her?

Person: *(Fighting tears of sorrow and rage)* She ended her life. *(With a final effort)* But that might have been her lack of faith.

Voice 3: *(Driving the point home)* Yeah, but it wasn't *their* lack of faith. The rest of them believed it! You know they did because you saw the faith shining in their eyes. Her own teenage son said, "Mom, I just don't believe you're going to die." You heard him say it! Well?

Person: *(Exploding, all caution and convention thrown to the winds)* Yeah, God! What about it?

Voice 1: That's better.

Person: *(Shouting angrily to the sky)* I don't hear anything! And I don't see any reason! But I want to know why! I'm a human. I'm a thinking person, and I want to know why! *(Showing more anger, voice trembling)* Why the drought? And why the war? And those poor little kids and Brian Wilson and Cathy? *(Jabs an accusing finger skyward.)* We prayed to you about that, and you never delivered! And you have the nerve to sit up there and watch that funeral…and listen…while Reverend Davies tries to make us all feel better. Telling us she was healed *(sarcastically)* "in ways we know not of."

What are you, some giant con man? You're supposed to love everyone. If this is how you treat your friends, it's no wonder you don't have many. *(Breathing heavily from the effort of the outburst, but calming a little)* I've always been too scared to say any of this stuff. At least now I've got it off my chest. *(With hopeless resignation)* At least we both know where we stand. *(Flopping into the chair, exhausted)* So go ahead and zap me.

Voice 2: *(Pauses, and then speaks tentatively)* So where do the prayers go?

Person: I don't know.

Voice 3: Maybe there's nothing.

Person: *(Starting up in desperation)* No! No, there has to be *something*.

Voice 1: *(Quietly)* You're too scared for there to be nothing, aren't you?

Person: *(Takes a deep breath. This is a big admission.)* Yes.

Voice 2: Well, that's it, huh? You're too scared for there to be nothing, and if there is something, you're scared it'll send you to hell. So you pray.

Person: *(Without any attempt at defense)* Yes.

Voice 3: Well, you have a pretty basic form of Christianity. When it comes down to it, you don't believe. You don't know; you just hope.

Person: *(Driven into a corner and not attempting to fight)* Yes.

Voice 1: Like a shipwrecked sailor clinging to a piece of driftwood.

Person: *(Fed up)* All right!

Voice 2: So why cling to it? Why not just let go?

Person: I don't know. *(Puts face in hands.)*

Voice 3: (*With a note of encouragement*) Yes, you do.

Voice 1: (*Conciliatory*) Dig deep. There's old Mrs. Anderson. Dear old Mrs. Anderson. She knows. She's sure. You saw it in her eyes when she used to teach you Sunday school. And Reverend Davies. He knows.

Person: (*Cynically*) Yeah, but that could be psychological—all in their minds.

Voice 2: (*Interrupting*) Oh, come on. You don't believe that, either. Down deep you've always known there must be something that makes people like that tick. And listen. What about Clarky? In and out of jail for years, and now look at him. Whole personality changed. And what about that little kid in the next town? A miracle, the doctors said. Totally…inexplicable…healing.

Person: (*Reluctantly*) I guess so.

Voice 3: So there's also that side of things that you have to take into account. *Something* must be working. You know, you're not so much a sailor clinging to a piece of driftwood. You're more like a sailor clinging to the edge of a ship and *thinking* it's a piece of driftwood. You just haven't climbed in yet. (*Pauses briefly.*) So pray.

Person: I don't know what to say. I've blown it, haven't I?

Voice 1: Well, if there is a God, maybe he's big enough to take it. Look, your own family gets angry with you. Do you love them any less?

Person: (*With little conviction*) No.

Voice 2: So pray.

Person: (*Pauses. Then makes an effort.*) Lord, Father…

Voice 3: (*Frustrated*) No, no! That's where you started before. You aren't ready to talk to God like that yet. You're not even sure he exists. You haven't gotten past the hoping stage. You have to start by asking for help. No show. No acting.

Person: (*Begins again uncertainly.*) God…

Voice 1: Good start.

Person: God of old Mrs. Anderson and Clarky and Reverend Davies…please be my God, too. Amen. (*Stands slowly, head down, obviously worn out. Slowly wraps arms around self as if cold.*)

Voice 2: So how do you feel?

Person: (*With effort*) Naked.

Voice 3: Congratulations. That's the first completely honest prayer you've prayed since you were 10.

(*Person pauses a minute, gives a faint nod of assent and, still with arms wrapped around self and looking very vulnerable, walks off. Curtain.*)

Strain Your Brain, and Stretch Your Faith

Do as many of these activities as time allows.

1. Have participants form groups of three or four. Assign one or two of the following verses to each small group. It's OK if more than one group looks at the same verses.

    Psalms 70; 77; Ecclesiastes 3:16–4:3; 8:9-14; Matthew 26:36-46; John 6:66-69; 2 Corinthians 11:23b-27

    Ask small groups to discuss what the verses say about pain, suffering, or doubt. How do the writers' experiences relate to our experiences in the world today? Allow time for discussion, and then have small groups report their thoughts.

2. Have participants stay in their small groups. Ask:

    • **When have you felt like the Person in the skit? Why?**

3. Have the whole group brainstorm about suffering, disaster, pain, or sorrow in the world and around them in their own community. List ideas on a white board. Listed items might include the loneliness of the old, the pain of the chronically ill, the hunger of the poor, the sorrow of those suffering war or separation.

    Have participants form groups of three or four and choose one item from the list. Have each group design a human collage to represent its area of suffering, using only their bodies and facial expressions—no dialogue or movement. Then have groups stand or sit in a circle, ready to form their collages during the prayer.

Read the prayer. As each area of suffering is mentioned, that group will form its collage. Write the prayer's response line on the white board, and have everyone repeat it after each area of suffering is named and collaged. (Feel free to adapt the prayer to suit local needs or to fit whatever areas of suffering have been specified.)

HONESTY
47

Group: Give us faith and patience, Lord, and in your love forgive our group. Give us faith and patience, Lord, and in your love forgive our doubting.

Leader: Lord, we are so human. We live in a broken world, and we are part of its suffering. In the pain of this world, we feel confused and lost. We pray, but sometimes we cannot see answers to our prayers. We long for justice, and yet the good suffer and die. We do not understand these things. Give us faith and patience, Lord. In some lands there is [name the first area of suffering, and have that small group form its collage].

Group: Give us faith and patience, Lord, and in your love forgive our doubting.

Leader: We see [name the next area of suffering, and have that small group form its collage] **around us in our own community.**

Group: Give us faith and patience, Lord, and in your love forgive our doubting.

Leader: We are horrified and sickened when we see images of [name the next area of suffering, and have that small group form its collage].

Group: Give us faith and patience, Lord, and in your love forgive our doubting.

Leader: Our minds recoil when we hear news of [name the next area of suffering, and have that small group form its collage].

Group: Give us faith and patience, Lord, and in your love forgive our doubting.

Leader: We feel the pain and sorrow of those involved in [name the next area of suffering, and have that small group form its collage].

Group: Give us faith and patience, Lord, and in your love forgive our doubting.

Leader: Dear Lord Jesus, you suffered, too. Let us never lose sight of that. You walked amid the suffering, and you helped and healed. As your people, let us take that responsibility wherever we can. In your name,

All: Amen.

Teen Freedom

And the Moral of the Story Is...

courage, freedom, mass media, peer pressure, relationship with God

Program Blurb:
The two high-trend and super-confident teenagers who stride onto stage are at a wonderful stage of their lives. They are growing up (well, in their view they've already grown up) and are living their own lives the way they want to…aren't they?

What God Says: Matthew 6:24-34; Luke 10:38-42; 1 Corinthians 3:1-3; Ephesians 4:13-15; 1 John 4:4-5

Handy Info: Freedom has always been a great catchword. Being able to think for yourself without having to kowtow to others is high on today's list of priorities. Teen media role models glorify the rebel figure. Those who obey or trust or follow are consistently put down as weaklings who can't stand up for themselves. One reason Christianity is so untrendy is that the basis of Christianity is unseating yourself and putting God in place as boss of your life. The world tells teenagers to get out there and not let anyone tell them what to do. They are told to throw off any form of authority. And there are plenty of people ready to help them do just that—or appear to do it—and it costs plenty, too.

Props and Wardrobe: No props are needed. Two teenagers should look very trendy. The other figures can be conservatively or corporately dressed.

Stage Manager's Clipboard: You'll need four types of music: contemporary, up-tempo rock or hip-hop; driving rock to suggest a high-pressure advertisement; the theme music of some well-known, easily recognizable TV show popular with teenagers (a good show would be one with a lot of super-cool role-model-type characters that teenagers might try to emulate); and a rhythm piece (participants might provide mouth rhythm, or a drummer can give the beat).

Before the group reads the skit, have people discuss the first question in "Strain Your Brain, and Stretch Your Faith." Then read the skit before doing the rest of the "Strain Your Brain, and Stretch Your Faith" section.

Cast List: **Teenager 1:** a girl who is very trendy and eager

Teenager 2: a guy with the same personality

Miss Tanya Verity Soap: a representative of TV imagery, done up like a soap opera character and somewhat over the top. She needs to be able to speak in rap rhythm when necessary.

Ed V. Tising: a representative of the ad industry, dressed as a corporate executive and incredibly smooth and confident. This actor also needs a good sense of rhythm.

P.E.R. Negative: also rhythmic and trendy, with a slimy sneakiness about him or her

Offstage Voices (any number): provide voices for soap opera effects, ad effects, and negative peer group effects. These actors need to be flexible.

Cue: Some of this skit is improvised or customized by the actors themselves, and it is here that they can get down to doing some good analysis of expressions, lines, expectations, postures, and behavior patterns. For example, certain sections of the skit have the two teenagers stir up those in the audience who aren't following the "accepted" mode of behavior. The actors should use the clichéd or well-known lines, insults, and expressions used by local and media cool groups to do this. They should also use cool walks and moves.

Cue: Stressed words in the song delivered by Miss Soap, Ads, and Negative Peers are in bold type.

Teen Freedom

(The stage is empty. Trendy rock music plays from an offstage source as Teenager 1 and Teenager 2 enter, walking confidently and smiling. They stop DSC, ready to address the audience. The music fades so their lines are clear.)

Teenagers: We just hit the big 16. It's the magic age. We go out to parties. We are computer literate.

Teenager 1: I'm taller than my mom.

Teenager 2: I'm heavier than my dad.

Teenager 1: I'm starting to think for myself.

Teenager 2: I want to make my own decisions.

Teenagers: The Bible? Christianity?

Teenager 1: Come on…that's indoctrination!

Teenager 2: It's a crutch for weaklings who can't form their own opinions!

Teenagers: I'm independent. No one tells me what to do.

(Music stops.)

Miss Soap: *(Enters SR.)* Hey, psst. Over here. *(Teenagers turn.)* Hi, guys. You look like two cool types. Independent. In control.

Teenagers: Who are you?

Miss Soap: I'm Miss Tanya Verity Soap, but you can call me TV Soap. And do I have something for you. You want to be even cooler?

Teenagers: *(Enthusiastically)* Yeah, man!

Miss Soap: *(Grandly)* Then watch this!

(She points out over the heads of the audience as if at a large screen at the back wall of the auditorium. The soundtrack from the well-known TV show plays offstage.)

(Offstage Voices talk, sounding muffled, to suggest the type of program the soundtrack is from.)

Teenagers: What is it?

Miss Soap: It's a TV show called [use the name of a TV show popular with teenagers]. Isn't it great? Watch it closely.

Teenager 1: *(Pointing at a character on the "screen")* Wow, she's really pretty.

Miss Soap: Check out the way she walks and talks.

(Teenager 1 copies what she "sees" and prances around the stage. It's great if she can actually imitate a well-known star of the program or a current movie star.)

Miss Soap: That's good. That's excellent!

Teenager 2: *(Pointing at a character on the "screen")* Hey, he's really cool.

Miss Soap: Check out his lines.

(Teenager 2 copies what he "sees" and swaggers around, shooting off a few super-cool quips with a dismissive, arrogant tone. He might also customize his performance so he is "being" some well-known star.)

Miss Soap: That's good. That's excellent! You can use these lines on teachers, parents, friends—anyone you like. And I have a whole set of attitudes and morals all ready. I mean, that's what life's about.

(The Teenagers rehearse their moves. The music stops suddenly, and the Teenagers freeze.)

Miss Soap: Hey! *(Pointing to someone in the audience who can take the joke)* Look at that guy over there. He's not copying. *(With sudden vehemence, like a general leading a charge)* Persecute him!

(Teenagers run to where Miss Soap points and explode at this unfortunate person in the audience. They improvise accusing the person of being a wimp and asking if he or she has any better lines. Miss Soap calls encouragement to the Teenagers. After a few high-energy seconds, Teenagers return to DSC.)

Miss Soap: *(Speaking rhythmically)* Good. Good. Just keep it up, and you'll be cool at work, at home, and especially at school. Remember, no one tells you what to do!

(Miss Soap steps back to USR as the Teenagers practice the moves she has shown them.)

Ed V. Tising: *(Steps on SR and calls to the Teenagers)* Hey, psst. Over here. *(Teenagers turn.)* Hi, guys. You look like two cool types. Independent. In control.

Teenagers: Who are you?

Ed V. Tising: I'm Mr. Ed V. Tising, but you can call me Ads. And do I have something for you. You want to be even cooler?

Teenagers: *(Enthusiastically)* Yeah, man!

Ed V. Tising: *(Grandly)* Then watch this!

(He points over the heads of the audience as if at a large screen at the back wall. Music and voices of a driving advertisement come from offstage.)

Teenagers: *(Excitedly)* What is it?

Ed V. Tising: *(Expansively)* It's everything! The right clothes—you have to buy that brand. The right music—you have to like that type. The right movies—you have to see that one. And you can own it all. I mean, that's what life is all about. So…go for it!

(Teenagers rush across to SL and start "buying" at an imaginary shop. They haggle and find the "right" thing. They try stuff on. They can use names of expensive stores and brands. Ed V. Tising yells encouragement all the time.)

(Sound effects stop, and Teenagers freeze.)

Ed V. Tising: Hey! *(Pointing to someone else in the audience)* Look at that kid over there. She doesn't have the right stuff. Persecute her!

(Once again the Teenagers persecute for a few seconds and then return to DSC.)

Ed V. Tising: *(Rhythmically)* Good. Good. Just keep it up, and you'll be cool at work, at home, and especially at school. Remember, no one tells you what to do!

(Ed V. Tising steps back to USR as the Teenagers prance around, showing off the stuff they've bought.)

P.E.R. Negative: *(Steps on SR and calls to the Teenagers)* Hey, psst. Over here. *(Teenagers turn.)*

P.E.R. Negative: Hi, guys. You look like two cool types. Independent. In control.

Teenagers: Who are you?

P.E.R. Negative: I'm P.E.R. Negative, but you can call me Negative Peers. And do I have something for you. You want to be even cooler?

Teenagers: *(Enthusiastically)* Yeah, man!

P.E.R. Negative: *(Grandly)* Then listen to this!

(Offstage Voices fade in, easily identified as teen voices laughing, encouraging, wheedling, cajoling, and insulting.)

Teenagers: *(Excitedly)* What is it?

P.E.R. Negative: It's called negative peer pressure. It's when your peer group tells you to do things that you know just aren't right. Not the things you all do that are healthy and fun and good. These are the others—dangerous, destructive things. And you gotta do them to be cool. I mean, taking a bit of a risk? That's what life is all about!

Teenagers: *(Excitedly jumping around)* We'll do them; we'll do them. *(Both talking at once over each other.)* Give us the orders. Where do we go? What do we do? Dope? Sex? Ecstasy? What is it? *(Teenagers can improvise here, naming a few topical practices or habits the audience will recognize.)*

(Sound effects stop, and Teenagers freeze.)

P.E.R. Negative: Hey, wait. Look at those two over there. They're standing up against the peer group. Persecute them!

(Teenagers again pick their target and accuse them of being gutless, scared, mommy's kids, frigid, and so on and then return to DSC.)

P.E.R. Negative: *(Rhythmically)* Good. Good. Just keep it up, and you'll be cool at work, at home, and especially at school. Remember, no one tells you what to do! Now let's put it all together. Are you here, Miss Soap? Are you here, Ads? *(Miss Soap and Ads leap forward with a "Yeah!")*

P.E.R. Negative: Then let's do it!

(Offstage mouth rhythm or drummer strikes up. Miss Soap, Ads, and Negative Peers can speak the rap in unison if they can make the words very clear. Otherwise, each should take a section. The Teenagers dance happily around, obeying the instructions in the song. However, as they move, their bodies gradually become more and more rigid so that by the end of the song, their movements are positively robotic and their faces blank.)

Miss Soap, Ads, and Negative Peers: Step **left,** step **right,** and curl up **tight.** Look **up,** look **down,** and turn **around.**

Now **follow** our **lead;** do **as** we **say.** We'll **tell** you **how** and **show** the **way** to **dress** and **talk.** Get **on** the **roll.** We **want** you **un**der **our** con**trol.**

Step **left,** step **right,** and **curl** up **tight.** Look **up,** look **down,** and **turn** a**round.**

Don't **care** about your **name,** what you **like** or **need.** Don't **want** you **saved.** Want to **see** you **bleed.**

Keep the **game** goin' **on;** keep the **sys**tem in **place,** no **in**divid**u**als just a **mask** for your **face.**

You're a **non**-**event;** you're **down** the **sink.** Don't **change** or **grow** or **care** or **think.**

Step **left,** step **right,** and **curl** up **tight.** Look **up,** look **down,** and **turn** a**round.**

We'll **tell** you **how** to **act** and **live,** and **when** you've **no**thing **left** to **give,** we'll **chew** you **up** and **spit** you **out** and **find** some**bod**y **else** to **clout.**

Step **left,** step **right,** and **curl** up **tight.** Look **up,** look **down,** and **tu-u-urn** a**round.**

(The offstage beat stops. Miss Soap, Ads, and Negative Peers slip off SR, leaving the Teenagers.)

Teenagers: *(DSC, speaking in unison to audience with robot stance and expressionless voices and faces)* We think for ourselves. We make our own decisions. The Bible? Christianity? Come on. No one tells us what to do!

(Exit robotically. Curtain.)

Strain Your Brain, and Stretch Your Faith

Have the group discuss the first question before reading the skit. Then do as much of this section as time allows.

1. Read 1 Corinthians 3:1-3 and Ephesians 4:13-15. Ask:

   • **What problem did Paul see in both of these Christian communities?**

2. Have participants form small groups. Have one person in each group read Luke 10:38-42 aloud. Then have the small groups discuss these questions:

   • **How are we sometimes like Martha?**

   • **What point did Jesus make to Martha concerning Mary?**

   • **How can we be more like Mary in our everyday lives?**

3. Have the whole group work together to come up with a list of the "have to do it" pressures that the media and advertising put onto teenagers today. Then ask volunteers to read Matthew 6:24-34 and 1 John 4:4-5. Ask:

   • **How can you avoid being "ruled" by the pressures we listed?**

   • **Where should you draw the line between simply enjoying being part of fashionable trends and being ruled by them?**

Lord Jesus, you walked in our world. You know its pressures and its temptations. Go with us hand in hand as we, too, face the forces of daily life in the media, in groups of peers, and in the advertising that surrounds us. Help us keep our heads clear and our priorities true as we live out the gospel in our families, schools, and workplaces. Amen.

Mike the Mechanic

And the Moral of the Story Is...

confession, faith, Holy Spirit, salvation

Program Blurb:
The skit uses a customer who needs to get the car fixed and the mechanic who does the job in an allegory of the process of being saved by Jesus.

What God Says: Luke 15:11-32; John 3:16

Handy Info: Two points in this skit are especially worth discussing. One is our inability to save ourselves, no matter what we might think. The other is that our commitment to Jesus is intentional and ongoing.

What does commitment to Jesus mean? Why do we need to invite Jesus into our lives? What is the alternative? These are all questions basic to any Christian's understanding of his or her faith. The drama outlines four basic steps to take to allow Jesus into our lives.

Props and Wardrobe: Actors should mime the car. The mechanic will need a wrench and a rag and might wear overalls.

Stage Manager's Clipboard: The customer can be anyone of any age, but making the customer elderly adds an opportunity to create a distinctive character. Good acting can make an elderly customer sympathetic, and the audience will love him or her. Change lines to accommodate a different gender or age group.

Cue: The Commentator can magically freeze the action and start it again by snapping his or her fingers. It's funny if the arm appears from the wings for the finger snapping. Little variations can be introduced where the Commentator forgets to snap as he or she goes off and has to come back on.

Cue: You might prefer to have participants make the car sounds instead of using the CD. There are usually a few "rev-heads" in the group who like to do car sounds.

Cast List:

Mechanic: down to earth, obliging, patient and practical. He wants to get the job done, and in the end, he does it for free.

Customer: basically ignorant about cars and at first convinced the car is fine. The customer's naiveté and ingenuous "dumbness" should get the audience to like him or her while sympathizing with the plight of the mechanic. (The skit is written for a female customer. If your customer is male, substitute "sir" where necessary.)

Commentator: drama-critic type who steps in now and then to outline the significance of certain salient points; well-dressed, well-spoken, well-educated, and given to gesturing to make the point

Set the CD to track 7 to provide sound effects of a car spluttering along and dying. **Track 8** provides sound effects of a highly tuned and powerful car starting up. **Track 9** has sound effects of a powerful car driving off.

Mike the Mechanic

(Stage is empty. Commentator enters from any side and walks in a businesslike way to DSC.)

Commentator: Hello. What you are about to see is not what it seems. It is a drama written in a very special way. It's called an allegory. *(Pointing to someone in the audience who can take the joke)* Do you know what an allegory is? *(Quickly, before the person can answer)* An allegory is a story that parallels another situation. It is a story with a hidden message. It symbolizes something. Everything inside the allegory connects with something outside it, and this thing within the story is actually the thing out there, which is…you'll see what I mean. *(Points to DSC.)* This is a gas station and car-repair shop. There is a gas pump here.

(Commentator quickly disappears off SL.)

(Mike enters SR, strolls to DSC, leans on what is apparently a gas pump, and starts to whistle.)

(From offstage right comes the spluttering car sound effects, from the CD, track 7.)

(The Customer "drives" on in a car that's on its last legs and pulls up DS, on the audience side of the Mechanic, who watches with a horrified expression.)

Customer: *(Climbs out of the car.)* Morning, young man. Fill 'er up, please.

Mike: Er, OK. Would you like me to check under the hood?

Customer: No, thanks. I had it checked last year.

Mike: Unleaded?

Customer: No, thanks. Diesel.

Mike: But this car doesn't take diesel.

Customer: Yes, it does. I like diesel.

Mike: Do you have the car keys?

Customer: What for?

Mike: *(Indicating where the gas cap would be)* To unlock the gas cap.

Customer: *(Takes a quick look.)* Oh, that's the gas cap. I thought it was here.

Mike: That's the exhaust pipe. Now, I'll just fill the tank with unleaded.

Customer: No, thanks. Diesel is my favorite.

Mike: But that's why the car is blowing out clouds of black smoke.

Customer: You mean it's not supposed to?

Mike: No, it's not. Are you sure you're not having some problems with this car?

Customer: Nope. No problems.

Mike: None at all? Ever?

Customer: Well, now that you mention it, for the first two weeks I drove it, it used to make a terrible burning smell. But I fixed that myself.

Mike: *(Doubtfully)* How?

Customer: I took the handbrake off.

Mike: *(Tactfully raises eyes to heaven at this. Then mimes opening the hood and lifting it up.)* It seems to roar a bit.

Customer: Now that you mention it, it does roar a bit when I'm going really fast. But it's the smoothness of these automatics. You can hardly feel the gear changes through second, third, and up to fourth at 75 miles an hour.

Mike: It's a manual transmission.

Customer: *(Busily going to get the manual from the backseat.)* Yes, I have a manual here in the back.

Mike: (*Grabbing the Customer before he or she can get any farther.*) No, the car's a manual. You've been driving at 75 miles an hour in first gear.

Customer: You don't say.

Mike: Ever noticed the engine missing?

Customer: (*Definite.*) No, it's always been right there under the hood.

Mike: No, I mean, is the timing off?

Customer: (*Looks at his or her watch.*) No, my Psycho Quartz keeps perfect time, but the other morning, when I started the engine, I did notice a big metal thing come flying up through the hood. What do you think that could have been?

Mike: A piston.

Customer: (*Greatly offended*) There's no need to use that sort of language!

Mike: (*Exasperated*) You don't know a lot about cars, do you?

Customer: I wouldn't say that.

Mike: Do you have a spare tire?

Customer: No, I'm on a diet.

Mike: Where's the jack?

Customer: He's back home mowing the lawn.

Mike: Ma'am, your car is a wreck.

Customer: (*Sounding knowledgeable*) Nope. It's a Ford.

Mike: There's a lot wrong with your car, ma'am. It needs fixing.

Customer: No, it doesn't. Anything that goes wrong, I can fix myself. I've already glued half a retread on the back bald tire.

Mike: Ma'am, admit it. Your car has had it. If you keep driving it in this condition, it will burn out, blow up, and break down.

Customer: Can I get a second opinion on that?

Mike: You don't need a second opinion. The car barely made it here as it is. Why don't you let me fix it?

Customer: (*Struggling*) Oh! Oh, all right. I admit it. The whole thing needs a complete repair and renewal, and there's nothing I can do about it. There. Satisfied? You made me say it.

(*Mike and the Customer freeze in position, and Commentator steps on.*)

Commentator: Hello. It's me again. I'll just jump into the drama at this point to illustrate what I was talking about before. Remember how I said this was an allegory? Well, look what has happened. The Customer just admitted the car needs complete repair and renewal. She faced up to the situation, and she confessed. Confession is the first stage of the process. Now let's see what happens next.

(*Commentator steps offstage. The Mechanic and Customer re-animate.*)

Mike: Well, you're in luck. I'm free and can do it right now.

(*Mike pulls a wrench from his pocket and prepares to start work, but the Customer grabs him by the arm.*)

Customer: Hold it. Ho-o-old it! Who's going to fix it?

Mike: (*Somewhat nonplussed*) Me.

Customer: (*Suspiciously*) Why you?

Mike: Because I'm the mechanic. I know how to fix broken cars.

Customer: (*Persisting*) But how do I know that? How do I *know* you're the mechanic?

Mike: (*Trying hard*) Well, look at my hands covered in grease.

Customer: (*Suspiciously*) You might be just about to put gel in your hair!

Mike: Well, look at my overalls.

Customer: Yeah, well, you could have gotten them from a secondhand store.

Mike: Um…well, I can show you my trade qualifications.

Customer: *(Forcefully, like a lawyer)* Could be fake!

Mike: *(Making his final try)* Well, I can get you to talk to satisfied customers!

Customer: *(Even more forcefully)* Could be relatives!

Mike: *(Frustrated)* Well, look, I can keep giving you all this evidence that I'm a qualified mechanic. But I suppose you can deny it all if you really *want* to. In the final analysis, you're going to have to trust me—have some *faith* in me.

Customer: *(Undecided)* U-u-um-m-m…

(Mike and the Customer freeze in position again as the Commentator enters.)

Commentator: Hello. Just a quick point. There's the second step. How exciting! First step: confession. Second step: faith. See? The hidden meaning. Back again later. *(Steps briskly off, and Mike and the Customer re-animate.)*

Customer: Oh, all right, I'll trust you. There does seem to be enough evidence for an intelligent decision. Um, can I help? I'm very mechanical.

Mike: *(Apprehensively)* Er, OK, you can watch.

(Mike goes to work on the "engine" while the customer watches over his shoulder.)

Customer: Ooh, there are lots of parts to a car.

Mike: *(Busily working)* Mmm.

Customer: What's that piece?

Mike: That's called the differential.

Customer: *(Savoring the word)* Differential. And you say it was really supposed to be at the back of the car?

Mechanic: Yes, we'll put it back there again.

Customer: *(Considering)* Can't understand why they didn't work. I used to oil them every day.

Mike: *(Gives a quick raised-eyebrow look to the audience and then stands.)* The whole engine is filthy. It's full of metal filings and oil sludge. We'll have to flush it all and cleanse the whole thing.

Customer: Yes, I suppose it could do with a cleaning.

Mike: Sure could. Especially the radiator. To get rid of all the tea leaves.

Customer: *(Embarrassed)* Well, it was a very cold day, and I was feeling a little poorly, and the radiator was boiling so nicely, I thought I'd make myself a nice cup of tea. *(Mike is aghast. The Customer continues thoughtfully.)* Did taste a bit chemical though.

Mike: But it's full of additives!

Customer: *(Big smile.)* Oh, well. I suppose that's why I don't freeze up on cold days. *(Mike is visibly horrified.)*

Mike: We'll have to flush it out. And we'll also have to clean out the air filter.

Customer: Suppose it is a bit blocked up.

Mike: Yeah. Those air fresheners you put in really made a mess, didn't they?

Customer: I just wanted it all to smell nice.

Mike: Well, we'll clean everything out.

Customer: *(Excited.)* Yes, clean it *all* out.

(Mike and the Customer freeze again, and the Commentator steps on.)

Commentator: *Well!* So the whole engine is going to be flushed out and thoroughly cleansed! What an interesting allegorical statement that is. First step: confession. Second step: faith. Third step: the thorough cleansing.

Now, 16 hours later…

(Commentator leaves and Mike and the Customer re-animate.)

Mike: (*Wiping his hands with a rag*) Well, there it is. All done.

Customer: Oh, it's looking great. All lovely and clean. Just like new.

Mike: Yes, it certainly does make a difference.

Customer: Beautiful. You've done a great job. All right, what do I owe you?

Mike: Oh…nothing. You can have it for free.

Customer: (*Stunned*) For free? Really?

Mike: Yep. No charge. All free.

Customer: But it took so long. And you worked so hard. (*Taking Mike's hands*) And look. You've cut your hands on the sharp metal pieces.

Mike: Oh, well. It's worth it to see it all fixed up and working properly.

Customer: Oh, well, if you insist.

Mike: I insist.

Customer: (*Climbing into the car*) OK. Fill 'er up with diesel, and I'll be off.

Mike: (*Suddenly leaps into action.*) No, no! Stop! Wait! (*Grabs Customer before she can get into the car.*) Not diesel. Diesel is part of the original problem. (*Customer looks dazed, not understanding. Mike tries again.*) If you put diesel in, it'll ruin all the good work I've just done.

Customer: But, but, but…I like the smell of diesel. And that deep, throaty roar makes me feel like the car's a truck! (*Makes a terrible roaring noise and mimes driving a truck, almost falling over in the process, and is caught by Mike.*)

Mike: No, you can't use diesel. (*Explaining*) This car is designed to run on unleaded gas. It's the right spirit for the system. And if you have the right spirit running through your system, you'll have better power and performance.

Customer: (*Interested*) Power?

Mike: Yes, the spirit gives you power and performance.

Customer: Power! You mean I'll be able to drag off that teenager who lives across the street?

Mike: Probably.

Customer: (*Excitedly climbing into car*) Oh, unleaded, please. Fill 'er up. Must have the right spirit.

(*Mike takes gas pump hose and begins to fill the tank. Mike and the Customer freeze as Commentator steps onstage.*)

Commentator: Well, there we have it. First step: confession. Second step: faith. Third step: the thorough cleansing. (*Speaking very deliberately*) And fourth step: the spirit that gives power. Wonder what that could symbolize. Let's see how it all sounds. (*Commentator stands behind Mike as Mike and the Customer re-animate.*)

Mike: OK. Take it away.

(*Sound effect of a powerful engine noise fills the air. Customer gives Mike and the audience a thumbs-up and is obviously very impressed. Sound effect changes to CD track 9, and the Customer drives off. Mike stands and waves and then freezes one last time.*)

Commentator: (*Steps out from behind Mike.*) Well, now you know what an allegory is. Interesting, isn't it? (*Points to original member of audience.*) And you'll be able to go home and tell all your little brothers and sisters you've seen an allegorical drama, and they'll all think you went someplace educational.

(*Commentator chuckles. Mike re-animates and is startled to see the Commentator standing right next to him. Commentator waves and exits. Mike looks after him quizzically for a bit and then shrugs and exits on the opposite side. Curtain.*)

Strain Your Brain, and Stretch Your Faith

Do as much of this section as time allows.

1. Ask the group what each of the following represents: Mike, the car, the gas, the cleaning, the admission of the customer, the customer's willingness to let the mechanic work, the cut hands, and the sharp metal pieces.

2. Ask:

   • **What psychological point did the customer have to come to before the mechanic could begin to work?**

3. Ask a volunteer to read Luke 15:11-32. Then ask:

   • **How is the son in the parable like the customer in the drama?**

   • **What specific things can you do to make yourself open to the word and power of Jesus in your own life?**

4. Have participants form small groups. Ask each group to think of another situation that could be used to show the saving work of Jesus. What else needs fixing up or cleaning? What could symbolize the work of the Spirit, the cleansing, and faith? If you have time, ask a group to do a brief improvised performance of its concept.

Lord, we praise you for rescuing us, for saving us when we didn't really deserve it, and for loving us enough to die for us. Let us always keep our focus on what you have done for us, and help us live our lives in gratitude and service to you. Amen.

What the First Christmas Might Have Been Like

And the Moral of the Story Is...
Christmas, human nature

Program Blurb:
This skit is really just about having fun with the Christmas story, but it does make you wonder... What were the personal circumstances of each person involved in that well-known story?

What God Says: Matthew 1:18-21; Luke 2:1-20

Handy Info: The Christmas story related in Matthew 1:18-21 and Luke 2:1-20 has been retold so many times that we tend to overlook the human element it contains. What problems and what situations confronted those who were part of its unfolding? Who were the shepherds? What sort of season was the innkeeper having? Who were the officials who had to organize a census of the entire Roman Empire? After all, humans and human nature tend to be similar from age to age. This skit explores the possibilities (with a little artistic license).

Props and Wardrobe: You'll need a clipboard, a pen, and a calculator for the Census Taker; a magazine and a large book for the Wise Man; and a dish towel for the Innkeeper.

Use Bible-times costumes, but add modern touches to suggest the occupations. The Innkeeper should wear an apron over his robe and carry the dish towel to continuously wipe his hands and wave around as he gestures. The Angel should have the usual white robe and wings, which can be a little lopsided. The Singing Angels should wear sunglasses and perhaps Hawaiian shirts. The Shepherds are definitely hillbillies and need large hats. Use big towels to make a turban for the Wise Man.

The Bible Reader can be on or offstage. If onstage, he or she can wear modern clothing.

Stage Manager's Clipboard: You'll need an offstage microphone if the Bible Reader is offstage. You can also have the Bible Reader walk on and offstage or stay onstage.

You'll also need a boppy drumbeat to accompany the Singing Angels' song. You might use group members doing a mouth rhythm or a drummer.

Cast List:

Bible Reader: official and well-spoken

Census Taker: busy, flustered, dissatisfied, with an always-picked-on attitude

Angel: a rather forgetful angel, not at all grand and glorious

Singing Angels (any number): definitely cool and rhythmic

Innkeeper: flustered and run off his or her feet, with any accent that works

Shepherds 1 and 2: talk and move really slowly

Wise Man: very wise, with an undercurrent of silliness

Offstage Voices: do animal impressions

Cue: Watch that participants doing offstage animal impressions don't get carried away and take over the show.

Set the CD to track 10. Track 10 provides sounds of a busy crowd (in the inn). **Track 11** has meditative Eastern music, and **track 12** provides the sound of a building collapsing.

Have the group do the first activity in the "Strain Your Brain, and Stretch Your Faith" section before reading through the script.

What the First Christmas Might Have Been Like

(Bible Reader reads Luke 2:1-2.)

Census Taker: *(Enters on opposite side from the Bible Reader if he or she is on stage. He or she is carrying a folder of papers and stands DSC, looking disgruntled. Complains to audience)* I hate this job! It never finishes. Count this! Count that! Look what they want me to do now! He calls me into the imperial throne room, and he says, "Imperial Statistician, find out how many people are in the Empire." Just like that.

And then, to scare me, he says, "Or you'll be thrown to the lions." Well, I guess I better get to work. The last Imperial Statistician got locked in a cage with [use the name of a well-known politician]. Got talked to death! So I suppose I'll have to go and start counting. Where will I start? *(Opens folder and points to what is obviously a map sheet.)* How about Gaul? No, can't stand the garlic. How about Egypt? Too hot this time of year. Let's take potluck. *(Closes eyes, and points to a place. Opens eyes and grimaces.)* Oh no. Not Judea. Why must I start there? That place is full of Jews. Not allowed to breathe on the Sabbath or something. Oh, well. Off we go. Better check I have fresh batteries in my abacus. *(Exits.)*

(Bible Reader reads Luke 2:4-6.)

(Sound effects of a crowd at the inn on CD, track 10.)

Innkeeper: *(Rushing around in a frenzy, furiously wiping hands with a cloth. Speaks to audience with a heavy accent.)* Mama mia! More people. I don't know where I'll fit you. The inn has never been so full. It's the census, you know. Come in. *(Calls offstage.)* Maria! More! Put them in the attic next to the other 16 families. *(Back to audience.)* Hello, sir. A bed for the night? Certainly, sir. Well, not exactly a bed, it's more of a cupboard. Yes. On the second floor landing. Well, it's better than sleeping in the street, especially with all those camels wandering around. You never know what might drop on you during the night. Yes, sir, sheets are in there. Supper at six. Mutton is very popular. *(Calls offstage)* Guiseppi. The kitchen orders are piling up. I have six more for mutton stew. Well, get some more. Try something. What about that big fat tomcat that hangs around the back door? *(Back to audience.)* Yes, sir. Up on the roof. Mind the pigeons. We need them for breakfast tomorrow. *(Exits in a frenzy to deal with some emergency.)*

(Crowd sound effect fades.)

Census Taker: *(Enters, mimes knocking at a door, and addresses audience)* Hello, I am the Imperial Statistician. Can you tell me how many people are in this house tonight? Yes, people. *(With enforced patience)* Yes, that includes Samaritans. *(Exits scribbling in folder.)*

(Bible Reader reads Luke 2:8.)

(Offstage sounds of sheep. Shepherds 1 and 2 enter dreamily, chewing on bits of straw. They stand DSC, staring vacantly out over the audience.)

Shepherd 1: A lot of sheep tonight.

Shepherd 2: Yep.

Shepherd 1: Any missing?

Shepherd 2: Two.

Shepherd 1: Where are they?

Shepherd 2: In the dip.

Shepherd 1: Which dip?

Shepherd 2: The avocado dip.

Shepherd 1: *(Nodding slowly)* Right.

(Bible Reader reads Luke 2:9-10.)

Angel: *(Enters and stands to the DSC side of Shepherds 1 and 2, who turn to face Angel and remain expressionlessly chewing their straws.)* Hello. I come with a message of great joy. *(Pulls out a small cue card and reads)* "To Abraham. Though your wife, Sarai, is a bit old and pruney, she will bear a child…" Oh, hold on. I did that one ages ago.

(Pulls out another note and reads) "Flee." *(Scratches self as reads.)* "Fle-e-e. For the Lord will destroy Sodom and Gomorrah. Do not look back or you will be turned into a pillar of Epsom salts." No, that's an old one, too.

(Searches in pockets or folder, muttering.) Should clean these out.

[If you want, you might customize another note instructing some well-known and carefully selected member of the youth group or church community to do something or stop doing something that everyone will recognize as that person's habit or particular feature. Be sure to be positive and encouraging!]

Angel: *(Finally finds last note.)* Ah, this is it.

> "Don't be afraid…I bring you good news that will bring great joy to all people. The Savior—yes ,the Messiah, the Lord—has been born today in Bethlehem, the city of David! And you will recognize him by this sign: You will find a baby wrapped snugly in strips of cloth, lying in a manger."

> Good, eh?

(Bible Reader reads Luke 2:13-14.)

(Offstage sound effect of a Caribbean-style drumbeat. The several Singing Angels conga line onto stage, join the first angel, and gather near the Shepherds. In time to the beat, and with line-dance or similar movements, they sing or rap through their message. Shepherds, totally expressionless, stand and stare.)

Singing Angels: Glory to God, glory to God, glory to God in de highest place.

Peace on earth, peace on earth, to all good guys of de human race,

From de mountaintop to de tropic isle, where de coconut palm and de sunshine smile.

I said glory to God, glory to God, glory to God in de highest place.

(They wave to the audience.) 'Bye!

(Singing Angels conga line off, and the drumbeat fades. The Two Shepherds remain staring blankly after the Angels.)

Bible Reader: And the shepherds were sorely afraid.

Shepherd 1: You see that?

Shepherd 2: Sure did.

Shepherd 1: You afraid?

Shepherd 2: Sure am.

Shepherd 1: Let's react.

Shepherd 2: Right.

(They both cower down and hold their arms over their heads, emitting a feeble and somewhat wobbly cry, which is supposed to be one of fear and shock but doesn't really have enough energy behind it.)

Shepherd 1: Right. I'm over it now. Let's go get the other shepherds.

Shepherds 1 and 2: *(Wandering off and calling)* Hey, other shepherds! You'll never guess what we just saw.

Shepherd 2: Yeah. We're all excited!

(Sheep sound effect fades.)

(Bible Reader reads Luke 2:15-16.)

(Sound effect of crowded inn on CD, track 10, fades in, supplemented by sheep sound effect.)

Innkeeper: *(Rushes onstage in a frenzy. Speaking as if the Shepherds are in the audience and waiting to be admitted to the inn)* Mama Mia. More people. *(Calling offstage)* Maria. Eight shepherds for one night only. I don't know where we'll put them. Put them in the laundry. Tell Guiseppi to get out the extra spare ribs. *(To audience)* What's that? *(Calls off again)* The shepherds have their sheep with them. *(Sudden inspiration.)* Sheep. Sheep…hmmm. *(To audience with welcoming tone)* That's all right. Pets are welcome here. *(Makes ushering movements.)* Shepherds to the laundry. Sheep to the kitchen. Yes, they'll be fine. Guiseppi will look after them. He's very good at handling meat…I mean, sheep. Yes, you'll see them again in the morning *(aside)* at breakfast. *(Exits.)*

(Sound effects fade.)

Bible Reader: Meanwhile…

(Sound effect of crowded inn, CD track 10 again.)

Census Taker: *(Enters and knocks.)* Hello, I am the Imperial Statistician. Can you tell me how many people are in this house tonight? *(Louder and slower.)* I am the…oh! Barbarians! Me count you. How many? You know? One. Two. *(Person being interviewed looks blankly.)* I'm not getting paid enough for this. This is *not* why I went to college! *(Exits in frustration and sound effects fade.)*

(Bible Reader reads Matthew 2:1b-2.)

(Sound effect of meditative Eastern music, CD track 11, fades in.)

Wise Man: *(Enters carrying a large book in which is concealed a magazine. Speaks with a heavy accent.)* Oh my, goodness gracious me. It has been wisely said by the ancient sage, "When great shining star appear in the sky…then you know…(dramatically) it is night time." *(Shakes his head in wonder at this amazing statement.)* Oh yes, very wise. Very, very, very wise. Must mean someone important has been born. I must check in my book of ancient astrological wisdom. *(Opens the large book and begins to read but then takes out the popular magazine.)* It says, "Your Stars for This Week: Gemini." That's me. "You are about to make a trip to the West to seek for a new king. And while you're there, watch out for old jealous kings, especially if their names start with H." *(Stops reading and muses.)* Hmm. A trip to the West. I wonder where we'll stay while we're there. *(Exits.)*

(Music fades.)

(Crowded inn sound effects, CD track 10, fade in again, supplemented by Offstage Voices doing various farm animal impressions.)

Innkeeper: *(Rushing on.)* Mama mia. What's this? More people? I'm getting to the end of my tether. *(Calls offstage)* Maria, I have three wise guys with camels and servants. *(To audience)* You have no idea what it's been like. I got 'em in drawers, cupboards, attics, pantries. I got 'em in sleeping bags hanging off the walls. It looks like a sausage factory. I even got 'em in the stable in the backyard. Don't know who's where. And now you want to come in, too? *(Calls offstage)* Maria. Twenty more. I don't know. Just put 'em somewhere. *(Exits.)*

(Sound effects fade.)

Bible Reader: Meanwhile…

Census Taker: *(Enters and knocks.)* Hello, madam. I am the Imperial Statistician. Can you tell me…eh? Oh, well, thank you. I suppose I am reasonably good-looking. What? Oh, I'm not really all that big and strong. *(Taking a step back.)* Madam. Hold on. Madam, I have a job to do. *(Retreats.)*

Bible Reader: Meanwhile…

(Sound effect of a huge collapse, CD track 12, combined with Offstage Voices doing various animal sounds followed by silence.)

Innkeeper: *(Rushes on in the last stage of frenzy.)* Mama mia. What a night! This is the last straw! I cannot stand it anymore. Haven't seen such a mess since [name of a popular media star] came to stay. The camels from the wise men divert off into the kitchen and run into the sheep from the shepherds. They all get the panic and stampede through the house and out. The roof collapses under the weight of the wise men's books. The tomcat stew is all ruined. The pigeons all fly away. What am I going to do for breakfast? I can't stand any more of this. *(Breaks into theatrical tears and gibbering.)*

(Census Taker enters and knocks. Innkeeper opens "door.")

Census Taker: Hello. I am the Imperial Statistician. Can you tell me how many people are in this house tonight?

Innkeeper: Aghh!

(The frightened Census Taker runs offstage.)

Innkeeper: What is going on here? What's so special about this night? Why does everybody have to come to me? All my Christmases have come at once…*(Pauses and then speaks thoughtfully.)* Hey. I have a feeling I just said something very significant. *(Exits thoughtfully.)*

Bible Reader: And that is what the first Christmas might have been like.

(Curtain.)

Strain Your Brain, and Stretch Your Faith

Do as many of the following as time permits.

1. Have the group think of all the characters in the story of the birth of Jesus, and list the characters on a white board. For example, list shepherds, inn guests, the innkeeper, census takers, wise men, and any other characters the group may come up with who could plausibly have been there at the first Christmas.

   Point to the list of possible characters, and ask:

   • **What would each of these characters remember as salient events on that first Christmas night?**

   • **What might have happened to them?**

   • **How did they each feel? Did feelings change as the night went on?**

2. Have participants form groups of three or four and choose one of the characters. Have small groups discuss what they might do and talk about if there were a "first Christmas night reunion."

3. Specify several stages in Jesus' life. Stages might be the time he spent on the road healing and teaching, the time just after he was crucified, or the time just after word spread that he had risen. Have participants keep the character personae they adopted for the second activity and, for a minute or so, improvise a reunion.

   Have participants form new groups so that each group includes several different characters. Describe a stage in Jesus' life, and have participants chat and share memories as they think their characters would. Then move on to the next stage, and have people chat in character again.

   Have everyone talk in character about two or three stages in Jesus' life, and then ask:

   • **How did you feel talking about Jesus from the point of view of someone alive at that time?**

Lord Jesus, thank you for the people who were part of your time on earth. Thank you for their humanity, their strengths and weaknesses, and their personalities. Thank you for being willing to come to us as one of us, to breathe the air we breathe, walk on the earth we walk on, and love as one of us. Amen.

Claiming Catalog

And the Moral of the Story Is...
faith, God's purpose, prayer, relationship with God

Program Blurb:

The customer has read the verses containing God's promises about having anything you pray for—only those and no others. And the customer has worked out a very profitable interpretation of those verses.

What God Says:
Matthew 7:7-11; Mark 14:32-36; 2 Corinthians 12:7-10

Handy Info:

Today in a consumer, "have it now" society, there is a real risk that people can come to regard God as a sort of divine vending machine, bound to automatically grant their wishes if they just use the right prayer formula. This perspective can lead to a very arrogant attitude ("I and God can do anything we want") or cause some Christians to put down others whose prayers don't seem to be answered in a very direct, tangible way. But most of all, it can lead to disappointment and disillusionment when prayers aren't answered in the way expected. This drama is obviously hyperbolic and lighthearted, but the issue it looks at is very real.

Before the group reads the skit, have participants do the first activity in the "Strain Your Brain, and Stretch Your Faith" section.

Props and Wardrobe:

You'll need a phone and several catalogs. If the Customer is to be seated, you might include a small coffee table and chair to provide a well-to-do atmosphere, but the Customer can just as easily be walking and talking on a cell phone.

The Customer can wear normal clothes, unless you want to make the Customer look rich, which might entail a classy outfit.

Stage Manager's Clipboard:

The Supplier can be offstage, in which case you will need an offstage microphone. If you want the Supplier and the Customer onstage, they should be on opposite sides of the stage.

Cast List: **Customer:** exceedingly confident and quite sure that all "claims" will be granted; can be of either sex, although this script is worded for a female Customer

Supplier: polite and patient but has his or her limits

Cue: The Supplier can speak in quite a correct and precise way, but annoyance at the Customer's persistent stupidity should become evident at the end.

Set the CD to track 13, which provides the phone sound effects (as heard by the caller).

Claiming Catalog

(Customer enters and sits or walks with cell phone. Punches in the number and waits. Sound effects from CD track 13.)

Supplier: Good morning. South Moreton Craft Supplies, can I help you?

Customer: Yes, I'd like to order catalog items 831, 5, and 115.

Supplier: Certainly. I'll just enter that in the computer. Are you paying by cash, check, or credit card?

Customer: No, I'm just claiming them.

Supplier: *(Unperturbed)* I see, is this a back order?

Customer: No, I'm just claiming them.

Supplier: *(Pauses.)* I'm sorry. I don't understand. Do you have an account?

Customer: No, I'm just claiming them.

Supplier: *(Taken aback)* But you can't simply…

Customer: *(Triumphantly)* The Lord says, "Ask and you shall receive," and if I'm simple enough to believe that, then…

Supplier: Excuse me, but…

Customer: We need to claim the promises…

Supplier: I don't really see…

Customer: The Lord wants us to call on him and receive the blessings of his bounty…

Supplier: But…

Customer: *(Snappy and parrotlike.)* God said it! I believe it! That settles it! Now, I'm claiming those things and trusting that they will be delivered.

Supplier: *(Firmly)* The order comes to $34.50 plus postage and handling.

Customer: I reject postage and handling.

Supplier: *(Stunned)* What?

Customer: *(With authority)* I bind all debts and invoices. I rebuke them, and I name them, and…

Supplier: *(Exasperated)* Look, lady…

Customer: And I order the demon of meanness to release your company immediately! *(With quiet confidence)* I will now go and wait at the front door and fast until my bounty arrives. Goodbye.

(Customer hangs up and picks up a catalog.) Now where's the phone number for that Mercedes dealer? Ah, yes, here it is.

(Customer dials happily as lights fade or curtain falls.)

Strain Your Brain, and Stretch Your Faith

Do as much of this section as time allows.

1. Have a volunteer read Matthew 7:7-11. Ask:

- **How might someone interpret these verses for his or her own gratification?**

2. Have volunteers read Mark 14:32-36 and 2 Corinthians 12:7-10. Ask:

- **What happened when Paul and Jesus prayed to be delivered from suffering?**

- **Why were their prayers answered the way they were?**

3. Have participants each find a partner to discuss what God meant when he told Paul that his grace was enough. Ask:

- **Why can this be hard for us to accept?**

- **What does the Customer in the skit need to realize?**

- **What pressures and attitudes in Western society make it hard to accept that God won't automatically give us what we want?**

4. Suggest that participants think about their attitudes as they pray during the coming week. Ask them to check each time that they're not approaching God with the attitude of the Customer.

Lord Jesus, you told us to pray in all places and times. Open our hearts so that we may pray with humility and gratitude. Give us the faith to pray to you as a child speaks to a parent. Give us the grace to accept your answers to our prayers. Forgive us when we pray purely for our own purposes. Amen.

Who Do You Know?

And the Moral of the Story Is...
courage, the Crucifixion, human nature, peer pressure

Program Blurb:

Peter denied that he knew Jesus. How could he do something so cowardly? But would we have done any better?

What God Says: Matthew 10:32-33; 26:31-35, 69-75; Luke 22:31-34, 54-62

Handy Info: So Peter denies his master. We all say, "Well, he really shouldn't have, should he?" But then we don't have the sound of yells and floggings and so on in our ears, knowing we could be next. Crucifixion wasn't uncommon in those days. At his age of probably mid-30s or so, Peter would have seen criminals executed this way. And here was the possibility of this torture staring him right in the face.

The disciples had previously proclaimed their loyalty and readiness to die. But when it came to the crunch, things were a lot starker in the dark of night, with the flames and torches, the swords and clubs. Like so many of us when we're put on the spot, Peter failed at the last minute.

Today, in a decidedly secular society, we might find it hard to admit to following Jesus. For teenagers this admission can result in being put down and socially blackballed at school and by friends. Media-created images of what Christians and the church are like provide a ready reference for those who want to put them down. Especially targeted will be those who express a real life commitment. And this is happening in a country that claims to be tolerant and where freedom of religious belief is a cornerstone of rights. In countries where Christians are persecuted by the government itself, the stakes are far higher. In this drama, we ask how loyal we would be in Peter's situation.

Props and Wardrobe: You'll need a handheld microphone (or a pretend microphone) for the quiz show host. You'll also need weapons for the Temple Guards and Soldiers and sunglasses for Peter and the Disciples. Make a fire by putting red cellophane over a flashlight.

Jesus, the Disciples, Peter, the Three Accusers, and the people at the trial should have biblical robes. Soldiers and Temple Guards could wear Bible-times robes or be dressed as modern security men.

Stage Manager's Clipboard: Divide the stage in half. The fire scene and the quiz show occur SL. The arrest and trial occur SR. Lighting on the SR side can be dimmer than on SL, which becomes bright and garish for the quiz show scene. The trial and crucifixion on SR are quite realistic, though done in slow motion. Having Jesus simply stand with arms outstretched is very effective.

Cue: You may have a drummer who can provide the rap beat for Peter's song using an offstage microphone.

Cue: You might lead a discussion of Peter's character before the group reads the skit. Mention the contrasts of courage and cowardice, Peter's desire to be liked, and his high and low points. He went from extreme to extreme and tended to be impulsive. That he had courage is not in doubt. After all, he was the only one of the disciples who actually followed Jesus after the arrest and went into the high priest's yard.

Cue: Stressed words in the song delivered by Peter and the Disciples are in bold type.

TRACK: 14, 15, 16, 17

Set the CD to track 14. Tracks 14, 15, 16, and 17 provide atmosphere-setting music, a rap or hip-hop drumbeat to back Peter's song, a burst of quiz show music, and a rooster crow.

PDF

The CD also provides PDF files of audience response cards that can be held up by someone at the side of the stage during the quiz show.

Before the group reads the skit, use questions 1 through 4 to lead a discussion about Peter's actions.

Cast List:

Peter: initially very confident and obviously the leader of the Disciples. His confidence is badly shaken during the questioning.

Jesus: he loves his Disciples but knows they will let him down. His smile is a sad one. He patiently and knowingly endures their raving before quietly being led away to be crucified before Peter has noticed he is gone.

The Disciples: clones of Peter, full of macho bravado; genuine in their love for Jesus but not prepared for the pressure

Host: full of fun, smiles, gush, and bluster; a very smooth talker

Natalie: beautiful, with flowing arm movements and a musical voice; the ultimate quiz show assistant. She and the Host seem cold and disconnected from what is really happening.

Crowd of Crucifixion People: includes priests, guards, soldiers, and crowd people; as many as will fit on stage and allow the audience to see what is happening to Jesus

Voice-Over: serious and sonorous to give the impression of an artsy, serious skit at the beginning

Three Accusers: slightly sinister. Their voices are ominous, and their gestures are slightly slower than normal so they seem more bizarre and threatening.

Who Do You Know?

(Stage is empty and dark. Lights are slowly brought up to a low level. CD track 14 fades in. Slowly, from both sides of the stage, Jesus and the Disciples enter, walking very slowly toward DSC. They should give the impression that it's going to be another one of those deep, slow, stylized Christian dramas filled with pathos.)

Voice-Over: On the night of his last Passover, Jesus went into the upper room with his disciples to celebrate the feast with them.

(Jesus and Disciples slowly mime breaking the bread and drinking the wine.)

Voice-Over: When they had broken bread, Jesus became sad and said to them…

(Jesus mimes speaking to the Disciples who in turn make "Shock! Horror! It can't be me!" type movements that are so super seriously stylized that they verge on the overdone. But it should seem to be a serious drama.)

Voice-Over: You will run away and leave me tonight. As the Scripture says, "God will kill the shepherd and the sheep will be scattered."

But Peter said…

(Peter stands forth from the Disciples as if he is about to mime the words, but suddenly the sonorous music stops. A bright light, preferably a spotlight, flashes onto Peter and Jesus, and a hip-hop or rap-type drumbeat, from CD track 15 or a drummer, smashes the quiet. Peter and the Disciples whip on sunglasses and begin to groove around the stage. Jesus quietly and sadly moves a little to DSR as the Disciples begin to party DSC and DSL.)

Peter: Hey, **come** on, **Lord,** whatcha **mean** to **say?** I'm the **one** who was **wit**cha **night** and **day.**

On **sea,** on **land,** in **wet** and **dry,** I been **hang**ing in **there** 'cause I'm **that** kind of **guy.**

I'm **big** and **strong,** and I'm **cool** in a **fight.** I can **mix** in **there** with a **left** and a **right.**

Let **any**body **lay** a **fin**ger on **you,** and they **wind** up **waitin'** in a **hospital,** too, 'cause **I'm** the **man!**

Disciples: *(Pointing to Peter)* Yeah, **he's** the **man!**

Peter: *(Pointing to Disciples)* And **they're** the **gang!**

Disciples: *(Thumbs to chest)* Yeah, **we're** the **gang!**

Peter and the Disciples: We're the **lads;** we're the **boys;** we **make** all the **noise.**

We're **with** you all the **way.** We're your **pride** and **joy,** and **no** one's gonna **split** us **up** or **down.**

Or **in** or **out,** or **'round** and **'round! We** stay **solid** when the **goin's** thin.

It's **one** for **all** *(they point to Jesus)* and **all** for **him!**

(The drumbeat continues as they swagger around being "the boys," high fiving, back slapping, being macho, laughing and hugging.)

Peter: Cast your **mind** back, **Lord,** and **you'll** re**call,** it was **me** who was **there** from the **first** "play **ball!"**

I **foll**owed you **right** from the **fish**ing **nets,** from **dawn** of the **day** to the **red** sun**set.**

I was **in** the **boat** and saw the **storm** go **still;** I was **on** the **road** and saw you **cure** the **ill.**

I was **there** when you **did** the Trans**fig**ur**ation;** it was **me** who **made** the great **decl**ar**ation,** 'cause **I'm** the **man!**

Disciples: *(Pointing to Peter)* Yeah, **he's** the **man!**

Peter: *(Pointing to the Disciples)* And **they're** the **gang!**

Disciples: Yeah, **we're** the **gang!**

Peter and the Disciples: We're the **lads;** we're the **boys.** We **make** all the **noise.** We're **with** you all the **way.** We're your **pride** and **joy,** and **no** one's gonna **take** us away from **you** after **every**thing we've **all** been **through.**

We stay **solid** when the **goin's** thin. It's **one** for **all** *(they point to Jesus)* and **all** for **him!**

(There is more backslapping and carrying on as the drumbeat continues. But over on SR, nasty things are starting to happen. Soldiers and priests come onstage and surround Jesus. Judas kisses Jesus, and soldiers seize him. The action is in complete contrast to the confident raving as Peter starts to rap again DSC totally unaware of the whole situation. As Peter raps, the Disciples one by one notice what is going on and, without Peter seeing, escape off SL, leaving Peter alone but still boogyin'.)

Peter: So I'll **tell** you what you **find** when you **look** at **me:** a **good** true **man** is just **what** you'll **see.**

I'm the **guy** who can **take** the **real** hard **knocks,** and that's **why** you **said** that I **am** the **Rock.**

I'm the **sol**id **rock,** and I **ain't** gonna **roll;** I'm **heav**y **metal,** and I **ain't** gonna **fold.**

I'll **stick** by **you,** and that **ain't** no **lie,** 'cause I'll **nev**er back **out;** I'd **rath**er **die.**

'Cause **I'm** the **man…**

(But this time there is no refrain. The drumbeat begins to fade or falter. The light goes dimmer. Peter looks around to see what's going on.)

Peter: *(With fading volume)* And **they're** the **gang…**

(Peter sees what is happening on the other side of the stage where the trial is now being silently acted out in slow motion.)

(From SL enter the Three Accusers, one carrying the "fire." They sit down around the fire DSL and warm their hands. Peter, having suddenly lost all his confidence, quietly goes DSL, glancing nervously at what is going on with Jesus, and sits down at the fire.)

Accuser 1: *(Staring and then pointing ominously at Peter)* Didn't I see you with him?

Accuser 2: Didn't I see you in his gang?

Accuser 3: Are you sure you aren't one of his friends?

All Three Accusers: *(All leaning toward Peter in unison.)* Well?

Peter: *(Looks left and right and sees there is no escape. He is about to answer when suddenly, again without warning, the lights become bright on his side of the stage. At that moment, the show music, on CD track 16, comes on loudly. Host leaps on SL in front of the fire group with a microphone in his hand and a huge smile.)*

Host: Hi, and welcome to TV's top quiz show, *Who Do You Know?*—the game where we find out just who your true friends are. And tonight we have a very special guest contestant, the big fisherman. Yes, it's Peter!! Say hello.

(Host whips up some audience applause.)

(Peter sits, stunned and obviously very uncomfortable, wincing at the bright light, trying to hide behind a hand.)

Host: And before we hit him with our battery of three questions, let's look at the subject of those questions. Yes, it's Jesus of Nazareth, who has just been arrested and is being processed right now. *(Points to SR)* Say hello to Jesus, the priests, Pilate, and their men.

(Again there is audience applause. The members of the Crucifixion scene, apart from Jesus, wave to the audience and then go back to their slow motion "processing" of Jesus, who remains deadly serious through it all.)

Host: Now for the rules. Get the right answer, and you get the prize. Get the wrong answer, and you hear the booby sound. And here it is. *(Sound effects of a rooster crowing from the CD, track 17.)* Let's hope we never hear it. But before we have that first question, let's see what the prize for a correct answer will be. Natalie, show all the people the prize.

Natalie: *(Smilingly enters SR and stands with the Crucifixion scene which by now has gotten to the point where Jesus is being beaten up by the soldiers. With a swish of the arms, she indicates what is happening.)* A correct answer on this question will get you a quick, illegal trial and a beat-up job from Roman soldiers and Temple guards.

Host: Well, let's get started. First question.

Accuser 1: *(Pointing ominously at Peter)* Didn't I see you with him?

Peter: *(Obviously terrified)* No. No, I don't know him!

Host: *(Sound effects of rooster crowing on the CD, track 17.)* Oh, dear. What an appalling start. But it doesn't have to stay that way. There are two more questions. What's the next prize, Natalie?

Natalie: A correct answer to the second question will win a scourging with a Roman whip.

(With a picturesque flourish of the arms, she indicates the slow motion scourging in the Crucifixion scene.)

Host: There it is. Now, the question.

Accuser 2: Didn't I see you in his gang?

Peter: No—I've never met him.

Host: *(Sound effects of rooster crowing.)* Oh, dear. Two in a row. But you know what they say…third time lucky. Let's see what the final prize is for the last question. Natalie?

Natalie: A correct answer for the third question will get you crucified with Jesus Christ of Nazareth.

(She indicates the scene again, and Jesus standing with his arms stretched out as the crowd gawks.)

Host: And here is the last question.

Accuser 3: You sure you aren't one of his friends?

Peter: *(Exploding)* Hey! I tell you, I don't know him!

(Sound effects of rooster crowing. The Crucifixion scene freezes into a tragic tableau.)

Host: And there it is. Three rooster crows. *(Peter, distraught, runs off SL.)* And there goes the contestant. Well, that's it for another show, folks. No winners yet. Three rooster crows, and still no one seems to know the man up there on the cross. *(Pauses and then points at the Crucifixion scene and stares intently at the audience.)* Doesn't *anyone* out there know him?

(Instant blackout.)

Strain Your Brain, and Stretch Your Faith

Do as much of this section as time allows.

1. Have volunteers read Matthew 14:22-33; 16:15-18; 17:1-8; 26:31-35, 69-74. Ask:

- **What do these verses show about Peter's personality?**

2. Have a volunteer read Luke 22:31-34. Ask:

- **How do you think Jesus knew this would happen?**

- **Why do you think Peter followed Jesus to the high priest's house? Did this show a measure of courage?**

- **Why did Peter deny Jesus?**

3. Have participants form small groups to discuss the situations in their lives that make it hard to be a Christian openly.

4. Have participants discuss these questions in their small groups:

- **How does Matthew 10:32-33 put us in Peter's situation?**

- **What do you think you would have done if you had been in Peter's place?**

PRAY

Lord Jesus, we love you and try to follow you, but you know how hard it can be for us. We're afraid of what friends might say. We're surrounded by forces that make it hard for us to be as loyal as we should be. Give us courage. Give us determination. Give us the strength to stand with you, even if it means others will put us down. Walk hand in hand with us every day. Amen.

Taking God Home

And the Moral of the Story Is...
faith, relationship with God

Program Blurb:
Two teens, David and Carlie, leave youth group and are picked up by their mother to be taken home. But this time they have a friend they want to bring home with them—God. What will Mother say?

What God Says: Isaiah 40:12-28; Micah 6:6-8; Matthew 28:18-20; Romans 8:35, 37-39

Handy Info: The issue of "not taking Christianity too seriously" is a real problem for churches, especially in the increasingly secular atmosphere of contemporary Western society. This gently humorous but powerful drama throws the situation into stark relief as God is seen as a person who comes with us into our daily lives. The skit offers plenty of scope for discussion about the reality of our faith in the everyday world, beyond the "official worship atmosphere" of church.

Props and Wardrobe: You'll need a large piece of paper with what appears to be a complicated diagram of interrelationships on it. You'll also need a handbag for Mother to rummage in. David and Carlie are typical teenagers. Mother is casual.

Stage Manager's Clipboard: The skit has no specific stage requirements.

Cast List: **David and Carlie:** curious teenagers; matter of fact about their relationship with God and convinced that he is a real friend and part of their lives

Mother: busy and needing to attend to important things; noncommittal about the whole religion thing and doesn't want all the Christianity stuff to "go too far"

The CD has the text of a responsive prayer, which can be led at the end of the drama. You can make copies and place them beneath the audience seats so the audience can read the prayer and be part of the response.

Taking God Home

(Mother enters SL and calls David and Carlie.)

Mother: David. Carlie. Over here.

(David and Carlie run on from SR.)

David and Carlie: Hi, Mom.

Mother: How was youth group tonight?

David and Carlie: Real good. Cool.

David: We actually got into some real discussion this time.

Mother: *(Half-interested and fishing in her handbag for the car keys)* So what did you do?

David: Well, we finished up doing this whole analysis of who God actually is…

Carlie: And the idea of a personal God actually being in contact with humans, like talking to them, relating to them.

David: Yeah, like it kind of blows your mind thinking that there's a God who actually talks to you.

Mother: *(Obviously wanting to get them into the car and home.)* That's nice.

Carlie: And we got into groups and had to draw our concept of God and humans in contact…*(Shows the paper to Mother.)*

David: Yeah, creating relationships and that.

Mother: *(Noncommittally glances at the paper. She has found the car keys at last.)* Very nice. OK. Let's get on home.

David: Are you and Dad going to church tonight?

Mother: No, not tonight.

Carlie: How come you never go? I mean, we go to youth group. How come you never show any…?

Mother: That's for adults to decide. Come on.

David: But why don't you just…?

Mother: *(Determinedly)* Come on. Into the car. *(She starts off toward SL.)*

(David and Carlie take a quick look at each other as if to say, "It's worth a try," and then turn to the Mother.)

Carlie: Wait a minute. There's someone we want to bring home.

Mother: You know the rule. If you want to bring friends home, you have to ask their parents first.

Carlie: We can't ask his parents.

Mother: *(Turning)* Who is it?

David: *(Pauses and then makes the big announcement.)* It's God.

Carlie: *(Enthusiastically)* Can we bring him home?

Mother: *(Bewildered)* What?

David: We couldn't ask his parents because he doesn't have any parents. In our discussion we learned that he's a pre-existent entity.

Carlie: *(Keeping the pressure on)* And do you realize that means he doesn't have any mom or dad? *(Sniffing)* He's an orphan!

David: Yeah, it's kind of sad.

Mother: *(Incredulous)* What are you raving about? You can't take God home!

David: *(Stronger)* Why not?

Mother: *(Definite)* Because he belongs here at the church building!

Carlie: But we could chat to him. Show him around.

Mother: *(Preparing to go again.)* Look. You see him at youth group on Sundays. That's enough. Now tell him to go back into the church building, please!

David: But Mom…

Mother: Look. You have plenty of things at home already to keep you entertained—a CD player, a computer, a brand-new basketball hoop. I know you two. You'll end up playing with God for a little while and then leaving him lying on the floor.

David: But…

Mother: We have enough mess at our place as it is. Besides, you can't take God with you. He belongs to the church, and other people might want to use him.

David: But the Bible says God loves each and every one of us.

Carlie: Yeah. He wants to talk to people!

Mother: I'm sure he does, but that doesn't mean we want him around our house all the time. Remember how we all got sick of cousin James that time he came to stay for a week.

Carlie: But this is different.

Mother: Look, I am not arguing anymore. Now come on and get in the car. I want to get dinner on. Dad and I are going to a movie tonight.

(She exits. Carlie and David confer, evidently frustrated.)

David: What are we going to do? We can't just leave him here.

Carlie: He'll get lonely.

David: *(Considering)* Well, he sustains the universe. He must be fairly physically fit. Maybe he could run along behind the car.

Carlie: Perhaps he could fly.

David: And we could sneak him in the bedroom window. And keep him hidden whenever Mom and Dad come near.

Carlie: And we could swap him from room to room.

David: We could get some friends to come. They could meet him. Make it a party.

Carlie: We'll put him on MSN. Tony and Rachel would probably like to talk to him. *(To offstage right)* God. Shhhh. Just follow us.

David: *(Looks around cautiously to see if Mother is within hearing range.)* But stay out of sight of Mom and Dad. I don't think they like you.

(Curtain.)

Strain Your Brain, and Stretch Your Faith

Do as much of this section as time allows.

1. Ask:

- **What is the mother's view of God and the church?**

- **What are some examples of her view that you've seen?**

- **Why might it be in the interest of powerful groups in society to keep God and the church "safe" and locked away? What are some of these groups?**

- **What are some aspects of Christianity that have been "sanitized" to keep them at a "warm and fuzzy" level so they don't get out of hand? (Christmas and Easter are two examples.)**

2. Have participants form small groups of three or four to brainstorm about common stereotypes of Christians, Jesus, pastors, and the church that serve to make them look comical, helpless, or irrelevant.

Allow a few minutes for discussion, and then ask the small groups to pick one stereotype to dramatize or illustrate. Groups might draw a character that shows the stereotype or come up with dialogue to act it out. Try to get a variety of stereotypes.

After a few minutes, ask the small groups to present their stereotype to the rest of the group.

3. Bring the group back together to brainstorm about ways to "bust" these misconceptions and stereotypes. Try to get very specific actions, and list them on a white board. Then ask participants to choose one action to do during the coming week.

4. Ask:

- **How can we make sure God is a "real" part of our everyday lives?**

Lord God, as we go home from this meeting, come with us and stay with us all our lives. Forgive us for sometimes trying to lock you away and put you in a convenient box. Touch every aspect of our lives and beings. Walk with us in our daily lives, and always keep us open to hear you speak to us. Amen.

Parables Mix-Up

And the Moral of the Story Is...
concern for others, God's forgiveness, God's love, obedience

Program Blurb:
Four parables—the good Samaritan, the prodigal son, the sower, and the lost sheep—are told all at once line by line, each line feeding from one parable to the next.

What God Says: Matthew 13:1-9; 18:10-14; Luke 10:25-37; 15:11-32

Handy Info: Parables are a great way to get a message across because they use images people can relate to. The parables Jesus used described situations that were familiar to the people of his day.

Props and Wardrobe: You'll need four chairs and four large books or folders to conceal the scripts. The four storytellers can be dressed in casual clothes, or they can be dressed as traditional Eastern marketplace storytellers with robes and turbans made out of towels.

Stage Manager's Clipboard: Place the four chairs for the storytellers DSC on the stage.

Have the group work on the first activity in the "Strain Your Brain, and Stretch Your Faith" section before reading the skit.

Cast List: **Storytellers 1, 2, 3, and 4:** all very expressive with plenty of "children's story time" energy

Cue: The storytellers can use scripts and read the stories, but they do need to make eye contact. Suggest that they highlight their own lines and use their fingers to follow the words of the person reading before them so they can come in smoothly, which is where the humor in this drama comes from.

Cue: If you want to involve a large group in the skit, you can add a children's story time audience. Any number of "children" can run in and seat themselves with their backs to the audience DSC, in front of the storytellers. They can measure their movements and responses to the content of the stories, but they have to be careful not to interrupt the flow. For example, the children might stare straight at each reader and turn their heads sharply in unison to the next reader.

Parables Mix-Up

Storyteller 1: A shepherd had 100 sheep. He knew all their names and looked after them very well. Each night, he would count his…

Storyteller 2: A certain man had two sons, one older than the other. One day, the younger son said to his father, "Father, give me the inheritance due to me when you die." His father agreed, and the son…

Storyteller 3: A farmer went out to sow. As he scattered the seeds, they went onto many different parts of his field. Some seeds fell onto the road, where they were picked up by…

Storyteller 4: A traveler set off on a journey from Jerusalem to Jericho. But on the way he was attacked by robbers and was left…

Storyteller 1: Sheep as they went into the fold at the end of a long, hot day. But one night, one foolish little lamb…

Storyteller 2: Received all the inheritance from his father and journeyed off to a far land, where he spent all his riches on wild living. But soon there came…

Storyteller 3: Birds that ate all the seeds. And some seeds fell onto rocky ground…

Storyteller 4: Bruised and bleeding and half dead. He lay near the road for a long time in the hot sun, and then…

Storyteller 1: Wandered away from the other sheep into the hills and got lost. The shepherd decided to leave the flock to look for the lamb who was alone in the cold and…

Storyteller 2: A terrible famine. He had spent so much of his money that he soon had none left, and all his friends ran away…

Storyteller 3: And some fell into thorns that grew up and choked them. But finally some went…

Storyteller 4: Along the road came a priest. When he saw the poor man, he simply passed…

Storyteller 1: Wind. So he hurried out to search for the little lamb. Through the woods, he pushed, and he climbed up steep hills until he finally discovered…

Storyteller 2: He was alone and poor. He went to work for a pig farmer, and he was so hungry that he would have been happy to eat the slop that was lying…

Storyteller 3: On the good soil. And it was those seeds that grew…

Storyteller 4: A lawyer coming down the road looked at the poor man, but he also passed by on the other side of the road. And then a Samaritan saw…

Storyteller 1: The little lost lamb trapped among the thorns. He picked it up and put it…

Storyteller 2: In the pig trough. "I will go back to my father," he said, and he traveled back to his home…

Storyteller 3: With 30, 60 times as much grain, and even as much as…

Storyteller 4: The poor man lying by the side of the road. The Samaritan took pity on him and got out medicine and poured oil and wine on the wounds…

Storyteller 1: On his shoulders and carried it back to the other sheep. And when he got home, he said to his neighbors…

Storyteller 2: And to his father. "I am not fit to be your son," he said. "Let me be a servant." But his father embraced him and called to his servants and said, "Quickly, kill the fatted calf…"

Storyteller 3: One hundred times…

Storyteller 4: And set him on his own mule. He took him to an inn and said to the innkeeper…

Storyteller 1: "Rejoice with me, for I have found the lamb, which was lost."

Storyteller 2: "For my son who was lost is found again."

Storyteller 3: Listen then if you have ears.

Storyteller 4: Look after him, and when I return I will pay whatever it costs.

All: And the message of the story is…

Storyteller 1: Just like the good shepherd, God never gives up on loving us.

Storyteller 2: God is always ready to welcome us back.

Storyteller 3: So listen to God's message and obey it.

Storyteller 4: Because God loved you first, you should love your neighbor as you do yourself.

Storyteller 1: Amen.

Storyteller 2: The end.

Storyteller 3: *Fine.*

Storyteller 4: That's all, folks.

(Curtain.)

Strain Your Brain, and Stretch Your Faith

Do as much of this section as time allows.

1. Have people form small groups of three or four, and assign one or two of the parables listed below to each group. Explain that each group could identify the main lesson in its parable(s). Then small groups will take turns briefly reporting to the large group about the parable and its main point.

Matthew 5:13 (Salt and Light)	Matthew 7:24-27 (The Solid Foundation)
Matthew 13:18-23 (The Sower)	Matthew 13:31-33 (The Mustard Seed and the Yeast)
Matthew 13:44-46 (The Hidden Treasure and the Pearl)	Matthew 21:28-32 (The Two Sons)
Matthew 22:1-14 (The Great Feast)	Matthew 25:1-13 (The Ten Bridesmaids)
Matthew 25:14-30 (The Three Servants)	Luke 15:8-10 (The Lost Coin)

2. Have people stay in their small groups to discuss Jesus' use of parables. Ask:

- **Why did Jesus use parables so much to make his point? Are the parables still relevant today? Why or why not?**

3. Have people work in their small groups to link four or five parables in such a way that their themes make a coherent message. Then have the small groups read or summarize the "new" parable for the large group.

Lord Jesus, you told many stories so that people could understand who you are and what your message was. Open our hearts and minds to understand your parables and the truths contained in them. Thank you for your love and concern for us. Thank you for being our shepherd. Amen.

The Christmas Radio Special

And the Moral of the Story Is...
Christmas, commercialism, mass media, secularization

Program Blurb:
Two commercial DJs are presented with a radio script about Christmas, which they are supposed to read to their audience. However, they consider the script too highly charged with religious elements, so they proceed to edit it. They end up with an emasculated, commercialized, fairy-tale version of the Christmas story.

What God Says: Matthew 1:18–2:12; Luke 2:1-20; John 15:18-19; 17:14-18; 1 Corinthians 1:18-25

Handy Info:

Of course, this script is very much like the feel-good stuff that circulates in a world that likes to sanitize Christmas. It's far better, it seems, to keep the story at the children's story level, all warm and fuzzy but basically gutless. The same treatment is given to the Crucifixion and the Resurrection. Very little is left of the smell of animal manure in the stable and the rough, simple shepherds who were there, to say nothing of the blood and drama of the Crucifixion and the amazement and human joy of the Resurrection.

This drama challenges performers and audience to examine both their own and the popular angle on Christmas and Easter.

Props and Wardrobe:
You'll need a desk for the DJs with a console of buttons, if you can find one. The DJs should also have pens, paper, and headphones. You'll also need typed pages that look like several scripts. The DJs should wear trendy clothing with some zany "celebrity touches," such as oversized sunglasses, a funny hat, or a loud scarf.

Stage Manager's Clipboard:
Choose some cool music to play on the radio program.

Before the group reads the script, have people do the first activity in the "Strain Your Brain, and Stretch Your Faith" section.

Cast List: **Jay and Jazz:** commercial DJs par excellence, smooth, superficial, and slick

The Christmas Radio Special

(Scene opens with Jay and Jazz behind their console being cool. Cool music is playing.)

Jay: It's the morning crew here on [name of town and radio station number], and this is Jay…

Jazz: And Jazz. We're looking at a fine day today in the [nickname of town], highs in the [customize to your own local climate, if necessary] mid-30s under sunny skies…

Jay: No wind chill to speak of.

Jazz: A good day to be on skis.

Jay: Or snowboards.

(The DJs can improvise about a great way to spend the day, mentioning local places and popular events.)

Jay: So how will you be spending your Christmas? We'll talk to a few listeners later this hour.

Jazz: But now, here is a special Christmas double play. Two tracks from the local band, the Infected Ants, off their new CD *Scratch and Itch*. [Substitute the name of a local band if you want.]

(Music blares.)

Jay: (Talking informally to Jazz off air as music fades) Did they give you the script for that Christmas holiday interlude we're supposed to do?

Jazz: Yeah, it's here. This is yours.

Jay: (Reading and recoiling) Uh-oh. It's a bit specific, isn't it? Do they know what they're doing?

Jazz: It's pretty religious, isn't it?

Jay: You're not kidding. Look at this stuff. Born in Bethlehem. Son of God. Came to save us from our sins! Where did they get this stuff?

Jazz: This is going to *offend*! You can't dish this stuff up to people at Christmas. It's like a church service! (Sounding determined) We're going to have to edit this or half the audience will be up in arms. We'll lose ratings like crazy.

Jay: (Grabbing a pen) Right. Think fast. What do they always say about Christmas? What do people like to hear? The safe stuff.

Jazz: (Counting on his fingers) Umm. Peace, love, giving, and sharing…

Jay: (Catching on and scribbling) Loving and caring, children, animals and cute things. The non-offensive stuff…

Jazz: [Insert name of well-known national politician.]

Jay: (Recoiling) Er, no. Offensive. Very offensive.

Jazz: (Agrees and goes on with the list) Families, parties, decorations, and presents…

Both: (Beginning to enjoy it all) Santa Claus!

Jay: (Romancing) The spirit of Christmas!

Jazz: Carols by candlelight.

Jay: Christmas lights. Cool. Good. (Finishes scribbling and then holds the paper out to look at it.) That should do it.

(Music fades.)

Jazz: Right, here we go.

Jay: (Slowly, in a smooth, cheesy voice stressing "special") Well, it's that special time of year again when we remember that peace and love are in everybody's mind and the season of giving and sharing and loving and caring is on us again at this very…special…time.

Jazz: And it's Christmas, of course, and Christmas, of course, is a time for children, of course, when children all around the world join hands and remember that very special baby who was born so long ago.

Jay: And who was that very special baby?

(DJs pause.)

Jazz: Well, *every* baby is special, right? So *every* baby is a *Christmas* baby…

Jay: And that's what the little drummer boy found when he played for the baby, because the baby was special just like me when I was a baby and you when you were a baby, too.

Jazz: And all the animals knelt down, and Ronald Duck and Michael Mouse and all the Walt Dizzy characters were there, too…

Jay: And the spirit of Christmas was there just like in the *Muffets Christmas Carol,* and that spirit is still in everyone's heart.

Jazz: So remember, all you need is faith and trust and that other special thing…

Jay: A little pinch of fairy dust…

Jazz: And you wish on a star…

Jay: And whistle a merry tune…

Jazz: And you remember your favoritest things…

Jay: And you believe, always believe, you always, *always* believe…in you because you, too, were once a special Christmas baby just like that special baby born so long ago.

Jazz: *(With high-power ad voice)* So if you want to phone right now, we'll take the fourth caller. And that caller will win our great Christmas giveaway…

Jay: …our beautiful, warm, and cuddly Christmas bear…

Jazz: …and when you poke his bellybutton, he sings a medley of traditional Christmas carols…

Jay: "Santa Claus Is Coming Around," "Jangle Bells," "Frosty the Snowperson," "Rudolph the Pink-Nosed Reindeer," "Whiter Christmas," "I Saw Mommy Hugging Santa Claus."

Jazz: And Christmas bear comes with a free pack of Christmas cards featuring pictures of sleigh bells, Christmas trees, presents, candy, and all the things that make Christmas what it is.…

Jazz: *(Laughing)* So at the end of our Christmas special, goodbye from Jazz…

Jay: And goodbye from Jay.

Jazz: Happy *X-mas* everyone!

(DJs remove their headphones and make it clear that they are off the air.)

Jay: Phew. Well, we rescued that one. Don't know what the scriptwriters were thinking.

Jazz: Yeah, people don't want to think at Christmas. They don't want to handle deep issues. They want warm fuzzies. *(Begins to read another script.)*

Jay: Yeah. Imagine trying to put religion into Christmas! What next?

Jazz: You think that's bad. You ought to see this rough draft of the Easter script they want us to pre-record. Heavy stuff. Here, look at this. *(Passes the script to Jay.)*

Jay: Mama mia! We'll really have to sanitize this. It's not safe for public consumption!

(The DJs get up to exit.)

Jazz: OK. So what are the things people like to hear about at Easter?

Jay: *(Counting off on his fingers)* Bunnies, chocolates, bonnets, parades, chickens, eggs…

(Their voices fade as they exit.)

Strain Your Brain, and Stretch Your Faith

Do as much of this section as time allows.

1. Write "How to Dumb Down a Christian Occasion" at the top of a white board. Under the title, write the headings "Christmas" and "Easter." On the left-hand side of the white board, list the following: "watering down the meaning," "editing the language," "generalizing," "linking it to popular culture," "inventing substitutes for the central figures," "using legend and fairy-tale replacements," "commercializing, holiday-izing, and party-izing the occasion."

Have participants refer to this list and brainstorm about common ways to water down Christmas. List them on the white board.

After the group has read the script, call participants' attention to the white board again and see if they have more to add.

2. Ask participants to look at the lists on the white board and think about Easter. Ask them to name specific things people do to reduce Easter to a "kids' holiday," and list them on the white board.

3. Ask:

- **How can Christians celebrate Christmas and Easter in appropriate ways?**
- **How can the way you celebrate be a way of sharing your faith with others?**

Lord Jesus, as we read and hear the well-known stories of your birth, death, and resurrection, take us to the times and places where these events happened. Let us see and hear and feel the events as those who were there felt them. Let us never water down the meaning and the emotion of what happened. Amen.

The Car Trip

And the Moral of the Story Is...
God's justice, God's love, gratitude, human nature, trust

Program Blurb:

This skit presents the escape from Egypt and the Exodus experiences in the desert as a car trip with Mom and Dad in the front and the horrible, complaining kids in the back. "God" is the driver. "Moses" is the mother who has to deal with the "Children of Israel."

What God Says:

Exodus 1:8-11; 12:31-37; 14; 15:22-25; 16; 17:8-16; 18:13-26; 19:1-21; 32; 34:1-6; Numbers 13:1–14:4; 14:20-30; 16:1-35

Handy Info:

The Scripture links and the drama present a good look at the Exodus—the patience of God and the ungrateful attitude of the Israelites. It seems to be human nature to kick against the very one who is trying to help. The Children of Israel did it, and we do the same when God's agenda doesn't match ours. Both God's patience and his justice are seen in the events of the Exodus. The drama will help your group understand the nature of a God who wrestles reluctant people toward ends that are for their own good.

Before the group reads the script, have participants do the first activity in "Strain Your Brain, and Stretch Your Faith."

Props and Wardrobe:

You'll need to set up chairs to represent the car, with as many chairs behind Moses and God as there are kids in the "car." You may be able to find an old steering wheel for God to hold. Moses should have a container of wet wipes. The actors will mime everything else. (No, you don't need to provide quails or manna.)

Make two life-size dummies by stuffing clothes with rags.

Moses and God should wear Bible-times robes. The Children can wear modern clothes but should look grubby.

Stage Manager's Clipboard:

Place the chairs for Moses and God DSC. The other chairs should be behind them in rows, but be sure that the audience can see the reactions of at least some of the Children.

Cast List: **Moses:** busy, flustered, continually annoyed by the stupidity of the Children but reassured by God's often unpredictable way of solving problems

God: always firmly in control and showing a good sense of humor

The Children of Israel: horrible, very ungrateful, prone to complain and fight

Cue: The Children can make plenty of noise at intervals, but they must be careful not to mask the words of God and Moses.

Cue: The skit provides a good opportunity to customize. Moses can continually tell someone (a prominent noisy member of the youth group or local community) to be quiet, sit down, stop annoying others, and so on.

Set the CD to track 18, which provides sound effects of car doors slamming and a car starting up and being driven. Turn the volume up or down where necessary to suggest the car going faster or slower.

Track 19 provides the sound effect of a huge splash as the Red Sea collapses on the Egyptians.

TOP 20 SKITS
TRACK:
18, 19

The Car Trip

(Moses and God enter, herding along a crowd of children. Moses and God seat themselves on the two chairs DSC, and the Children crowd onto the seats behind them.)

(Play sound effects of car doors slamming and car starting on CD track 18. God holds his hands up as though holding a steering wheel.)

Moses: OK, Children of Israel, in you get. Come on, into the backseat. Yes, that's right, all 600,000 of you.

God: Moses, you'd better get them moving or the Egyptians will be on us.

Moses: Come on. Finish off that unleavened bread. Yes, I know it's tough. And don't take too much Egyptian gold and jewels with you or we won't fit it in.

God: Right. Let's get moving. We'll head south to Succoth and then swing north to Zephon and the Sea of Reeds.

Moses: OK, God. You're the driver. Do we stop at Zephon?

God: No. It's too small.

Moses: How small?

God: We just passed it.

Moses: Oh. *(Looking out the back window)* Uh-oh. We're being followed. Look in the rearview mirror.

God: The Egyptians. I thought so. OK, now, let's see.

Moses: Hurry, Lord. They're faster. This is only an Exodus series family sedan.

God: OK, Moses. Don't panic. I have an idea. I'll swing east here.

Moses: But there's nothing in that direction but a big swamp full of papyrus reeds.

God: I know what I'm doing.

Moses: *(Turning to the back)* Look, be quiet, you kids. Sit down. I know we're being followed, so keep your heads inside. And stop throwing those fruit peels out the window. Do you want us stopped for littering?

God: Moses, you take the wheel for a moment. Just keep going straight ahead.

Moses: *(Uncertainly)* You sure? Into the water?

God: Yep, go for it. *(God becomes very still and stares as if concentrating hard on something.)*

Moses: You kids keep quiet. I can't concentrate. OK, here we go. Hold your breath! *(Takes a deep breath and braces as if for an impact, and then suddenly relaxes.)* Hey. The water's gone!

God: Good one, eh? *(Takes the wheel again.)*

Moses: Unreal! Nice one, Lord. Hey, how about that, kids? No, we cannot stop for a look. Just hang on.

God: There, now look in the rearview mirror. *(Bends it to Moses' side.)*

Moses: Here come the Egyptians in their souped-up [insert name of popular car]. Hey, they're getting bogged down in the mud. *(Laughs, and then suddenly flinches.)*

(Sound effects of huge splash, CD track 19.)

Moses: Wow! Look at that! Sort of like a giant car wash.

God: We'll keep going ahead here and then swing south.

Moses: Right. *(To the Children in the back)* Be quiet in the back! Leave the door handles alone.

God: OK, this is it. The desert of Shur.

Moses: *(To the Children in the back)* Yes, I know it's hot. Here, have a wet wipe. And open the windows. And get your feet out of the back of my seat. It's uncomfortable.

God: Now what's wrong?

Moses: They're thirsty. *(To the Children in the back)* All right, all right!

God: Give them the water bottle.

Moses: Here's some water. Oh, what's wrong now?

God: Now what's up?

Moses: They say it tastes bitter! Should we stop?

God: No. There's a little piece of wood in the glove compartment. Tell them to put that in the water. The water will taste better.

Moses: *(Turning back)* Here, you kids. Put this in the water, and it'll be nice again. I don't know why; just do it!

God: Right. We turn here and keep on south for Sinai. It'll be a long haul. What did that sign say back there?

Moses: The Wilderness of Sin.

God: Good. We're on track, strange as that may sound.

Moses: *(To the Children in the back)* Keep quiet, back there. *(Pauses as if listening.)* Well, give it back. She had it first. *(To God)* They're getting cranky because they're hungry.

God: OK, OK. We can eat in a bit.

Moses: *(To the Children in the back)* No, you can't have it right now. *(To God)* Can we give them something? It's miles to the next stop.

God: All right. *(Louder, to the Children)* OK, kids. Get ready. There—it's raining food inside the car. It's called manna. Tastes like lollipops!

Moses: Yes, it is yummy! All say, "Thank you, God." That's better. Now don't stash it. Just eat it now. Oh, yuck! I did tell you not to put it in your pockets, didn't I? *(Pauses briefly.)* Yes, give it to me, and I'll put it in the trash bag.

(Turns toward the front.) There. That should keep them quiet for a bit.

God: Can't you guys chew a little more quietly?

Moses: *(To the Children in the back)* Yes, I know it's sticky. Here's a wet wipe. *(Pauses briefly.)* What? *(Pauses briefly.)* Oh, aren't you kids ever satisfied?

God: Now what?

Moses: They say they're sick of manna. They want some meat to eat.

God: What sort of meat?

Moses: *(Turns to get Children's opinions and then turns to front.)* Fried chicken.

God: OK, then.

Moses: But there isn't a place within miles.

God: No problem. Colonel God will provide it. Tell the children to watch the windows.

Moses: OK, kids. Watch the windows and…*(Ducks violently.)* Aghh! Quails! Millions of quails. They just flew in the window!

God: Yep. They're migrating through here. Nice timing, eh?

Moses: Amazing. Right when we needed them. *(To the Children in the back)* Quick. Grab 'em! Kill 'em! Put some on the back window ledge to preserve them. The rest you can cook and eat. Keep your fires on the floor, and don't let them get too big. Here's a wet wipe. No, don't try to cook it!

God: Are they happy now?

Moses: For a while, anyway. Hey. Who's that on the road ahead?

God: Amalekites. Tough bunch. They'll probably want to fight.

Moses: *(To the Children)* OK, kids. Here, each of you take a handful of that rotten manna. Yes, watch out for the maggots. Got it ready? Now when I say "go," you throw it out the windows.

God: Get ready. I'll give you a good shot. Now! *(Swerves the car a bit.)*

Moses: *(To the Children)* Go! Oh! Right in the head. They'll be cleaning that off for ages. Here are some wet wipes for your hands. No, don't eat them. Stop it. Quiet! Please be quiet.

God: Now what?

Moses: They're fighting. *(To the Children in the back)* I said "be quiet" or there'll be an accident. *(Pauses briefly.)* Well, you give it back. *(Pauses briefly.)* I don't care if he had it first. *(Turns to front.)* Oh, God, I can't do all this by myself.

God: Well, pick some of the older ones to be judges.

Moses: Good idea. *(To the Children in the back)* Aaron, you and your friends, you're oldest. You coordinate it. Do it quietly, please. There's no need for all that fuss. *(Turns to front.)* Oh, they still need help.

God: Look, here's Mount Sinai. I'll pull over. Now let's work out some basic rules.

Moses: OK. *(To the Children in the back)* Aaron, you supervise while God gives me these instructions. *(Turns back to front to watch God.)*

God: *(Mimes scribbling on some paper.)* Right, now you take these. Then turn around and have a look. I have a feeling that all is not well back at the farm.

Moses: *(Turns to the Children in the back)* Right. Here are some rules. Ten basic rules for… *What's this?*

God: What's wrong?

Moses: *(To God)* I don't believe this. That souvenir we picked up at the Big Golden Cow. They've set it up, and they're worshipping it!

(Turns to the Children in the back.) How many times do I have to tell you not to worship other gods? Aaron, you ought to know better! *(Pauses briefly.)* I don't care if they made you do it! Sometimes I get so frustrated with you that I could…*(Mimes tearing up the paper in a rage.)* Now you take that golden calf and eat it! Yes, go on, all of it. And promise not to do it again. Now I'm going to get some more rules, and this time you better behave while I'm away.

God: *(Mimes passing a paper to Moses.)* Here's a second set. I made a copy in case. And here's a whole book of ceremonial law for them to read and color in. Plus an ark-of-the-covenant kit with instructions on how to put it together. And a wet wipe.

Moses: Right. *(Turns to the Children in the back.)* Here are some activities to help you behave. And don't fight over them. Yes, I know my face is shining. That's because I am getting *very, very angry!*

God: Well, here we are—the Promised Land Caravan Park. I'll just drive around the block while you figure out what to do.

Moses: What would you suggest?

God: Well, you could send in some spies to case the joint and report back.

Moses: OK. *(Turns to the Children in the back.)* You 12, jump out here, and we'll pick you up next time 'round the block.

(God continues to drive as Moses faces front. After a moment of silence…)

Moses: *(To God)* I wonder how they'll do.

God: I have a feeling I know already.

Moses: Here they are. OK. Jump in. Tell us all about it. Shhh. One at a time.

God: Well?

Moses: *(Sighs with frustration as he turns back to God again.)* They're all too scared to go into the Promised Land Caravan Park. They say there are a lot of big kids in the recreation room who might beat them up. Only two say we can do it because you're with us.

God: That's what I was afraid they'd say. I am getting a little tired of these children.

Moses: Not only that, but they want to choose a new leader and go back to Egypt. *(Turning to Children)* Keep quiet! We can't talk!

God: What? More complaining? After all I've done for them? I got them out of Egypt. Protected them. Fed them. Gave them wet wipes. And this is the faith they have in me?

Moses: *(After listening to the rumblings in the back)* And now, Korah the Levite and some others are saying I'm going too far and setting myself above the rest of them.

God: Right. That's it! *(Calling out)* I'm coming into the backseat myself to let you kids have it!

Moses: No, Lord! You're driving. Don't let go of the wheel, please.

God: Well, I've had enough of this mob. *(Calling out)* Anyone on Korah's side, move over to the right side of the backseat. The rest of you, get out of the way.

Moses: *(Looking back at the Children)* Lord, why did you ask Korah and the rebels to move to the right-hand side of the seat?

God: Because that's where the ejection spring is.

(God makes a lever-pulling movement. Children throw stuffed dummies offstage, or a couple of the Children can simply run offstage.)

Moses: *(Turning back to God)* They're quiet now.

God: Well, it's a bit late now! I've had it with this generation! We're getting off this block circuit and going back into the wilderness.

Moses: *(To the Children)* Stop complaining! It's your fault it happened.

God: *(Calling to Children)* So you weren't satisfied with the Promised Land Caravan Park, eh? Even with its nice kiosks with big bunches of grapes and milk and honey. Well, we'll have a look at a few other places. We'll take a 40-year tour through the wilderness. Maybe then you'll appreciate the Promised Land.

Moses: *(To the Children)* Be quiet! I think it's going to be a long trip. We aren't going to stop until you can behave yourselves. No, you can't have a wet wipe!

(Lights fade and curtain, or God, Moses, and the Children exit the stage either side in formation so it looks like they're driving off.)

Strain Your Brain, and Stretch Your Faith

1. Show participants a map of the Middle East in Bible times (from a Bible or concordance or from the Internet) so they can see the general layout of Egypt, the Red Sea, and the Promised Land. Ask volunteers to tell parts of the Exodus story, and be ready to fill in as necessary. The general framework of the story is in the "What God Says" Scripture verses.

Then have the group discuss these questions:

- **What types of complaints did Moses and God have to deal with?**

- **How did the Israelites show their fickleness and lack of trust?**

- **In what special ways did God provide for their material and social needs?**

2. Have participants form small groups to discuss the following questions.

- **Why did the Children of Israel complain so much?**

- **When the Children of Israel complained about being hungry, God provided food. But when they complained about big kids in the Promised Land Caravan Park, God punished them. Why do you think the different complaints brought such different consequences?**

- **What do you complain to God about? What do your complaints reveal about your trust in God?**

3. Ask participants to think about their lives—about friends, school, and plans for the future. Ask them to consider what's most important and where they're struggling. Allow a minute or so for people to think. Then ask:

- **What would it look like to "give God the wheel" in each important part of your life?**

- **In what area of your life is it easiest to "give God the wheel?" Where is it most difficult?**

4. Ask everyone to think of one area in his or her life where it's difficult to give God control. Ask participants to silently imagine giving God control and then commit to following through during the coming week.

Lord God, you led Israel out of Egypt and continued to support them even after they had disobeyed and disowned you. Thank you for your forgiveness of our own disobedience. Teach us to trust you and follow you no matter what, even when the going gets tough. Give us the grace and the strength to hold your hand and let you lead us where you will. Amen.

THE Elijah Tag Team

And the Moral of the Story Is...
courage, faith, God's justice, God's protection, persecution

Program Blurb:
A match between the white team, including the prophets Elijah (1 Kings 18:1), Micaiah (1 Kings 22:6-14), and Elisha (1 Kings 19:19-21), all coached by God and supporters such as Obadiah (1 Kings 18:1-4), and the red team of King Ahab, Queen Jezebel, and their false prophets.

What God Says: 1 Kings 16:29-33; 17:1-7; 18:1–22:40

Handy Info: Teenagers who stand up for their faith against criticism can take a lot of encouragement from figures such as Elijah, Obadiah, and Micaiah. So if there are a few in your group who have never heard of these prophets, this drama will show them that brave people have always been prepared to stand up against corrupt political and moral institutions. King Ahab and Queen Jezebel rate high among the worst rulers in the Old Testament. On the other hand, Elijah rates as one of history's toughest prophets. And with God on his side, the stage is set for the sparks to fly.

Read the "What God Says" Scripture passages so you can summarize them before your group reads the script. You many want to choose specific passages to have volunteers read aloud.

Cue: You can insert your own customizing touches regarding Jezebel's makeup practices. In 2 Kings 9:30, the Bible specifically mentions her use of makeup (which was a common enough practice for women in those days, especially wealthy ones). Each time the script mentions her makeup, you can insert a short one- or two-sentence ad of your own devising that has Jezebel or her servants recommend a makeup product, basing the ad on a current TV makeup ad, if you like.

Cue: You might want to suggest a wrestling arena atmosphere with onstage characters on each side cheering for their champions, groaning and slapping their foreheads when something goes wrong and giving high fives and waving their fists in the air when their side wins a point.

Cue: The Commentators give cues to the actors as they describe the action on stage.

Cast List:

Commentators 1 and 2: energetic and enthusiastic sportscasters. The commentators can read their lines from offstage.

Elijah: alternates between being a grandly ferocious prophet and being totally scared

Micaiah: a confident prophet who believes God is with him

Ahab: henpecked, sniveling, nasty, and cowardly

Jezebel: dominating, evil, determined, totally controlling her husband

Obadiah: a palace official who wants to do the right thing and is prepared to defy the royals to do it

God: the coach of his team, constantly encouraging, energetically supporting, and calling out tips

Naboth: helpless, inoffensive, and doomed

Jehu: fierce and determined; doesn't like Jezebel at all

False Prophets (any number): fanatical and energetic

True Prophets (any number): loyal and brave

Soldiers and Servants (any number): ready to follow orders

People of Israel (any number): fickle and easily awed

Ravens

Props and Wardrobe:

You'll need a loaf of bread, a water bottle, a large red cloth, and an umbrella, as well as a bell (to ring at the start of the action) and spears and swords if you want the soldiers to be armed.

The Commentators should wear modern clothes, and the three Prophets should wear Bible-times robes. The False Prophets should wear weird magical outfits. The King and Queen should have robes and crowns. Jezebel might wear heavy makeup. The Ravens should dress in black and might also have something to suggest wings.

Stage Manager's Clipboard:

The stage doesn't need to have an actual ring or enclosure on it.

Set the CD to track 20, which provides 45 seconds of loud cheering so it can be faded in and out each time the God team wins.

PDF: The CD also provides PDFs of signs to be held up by members of opposing teams and members of the audience to encourage a live-event atmosphere.

THE Elijah Tag Team

(The stage is divided into two halves, one for the white God team and one for the red Ahab team. Teams keep to their sides of the stage, leaving center stage to be the "ring" into and out of which they can leap to do the "fighting." While fighters are in the ring, each team provides cheering, back slapping, rubdowns, and so on.)

(Fade in crowd sounds from CD track 20 whenever you please.)

Commentator 1: Here we are at the tag team match: God versus the forces of evil.

Commentator 2: In the white corner, the God team comprises Elijah, that fearless prophet; the prophet Micaiah; Elisha, Elijah's young assistant; Obadiah, servant of King Ahab; and finally, as coach, God.

Commentator 1: And in the red corner, King Ahab. Worst king Israel ever had. Self-centered, cruel, fickle—and those are his good points. He is supported by his army and false prophets. Coaching their team is his wife, Jezebel, queen of Israel, worshipper of the false god Baal, ruthless [insert brand name] beauty products lady.

Commentator 2: Well, the fighters are in their corners, and *(sound effects of a bell ringing)* it's on. *(Jezebel and Ahab enter the ring.)* What's this? An illegal move. The red team has the coach in the ring, too. And here's their first blow.

Jezebel: I want shrines and sacrifices to the god Baal built all over the place.

Ahab: Yes, dear.

Jezebel: I want the worship of the Lord out. In fact, I want it wiped out.

Ahab: *(Pauses. Gulps.)* Yes, my sweet. Anything you say.

(Jezebel and Ahab withdraw to their side of the stage to applause from their own team. Jezebel withdraws to the far side of the team to do her face.)

Commentator 1: Wow, a massive blow dealt out by the red team. Ahab sits back and relaxes. Jezebel puts on makeup. Looks like the worship of the true God is in real trouble.

(Elijah leaps into the ring.)

Commentator 2: And here is the God team. It's Elijah, ready for battle!

(Elijah begins to stride over to the other side, right up to Ahab's face.)

Commentator 2: And just look at this.

Commentator 1: Yes, this is typical of the audacity of the God team. Elijah is striding right up to the palace of the king. The king is too stunned to move.

Ahab: *(His jaw drops.)* I'm too stunned to move. *(Glances desperately around.)*

Commentator 2: He needs his coach, but she's busy putting on moisturizer.

Elijah: You want to follow false gods? Right! God says there will be no rain for two or three years! *(Strides back to his own side, where he is rubbed down and cheered.)*

Ahab: Dear, dear. What should I do? Er…arrest him someone.

Commentator 1: But it's too late. Elijah is gone, and the queen will not be impressed.

Jezebel: *(Returns to the front of the team with Ahab.)* What's going on?

Ahab: *(In a panic)* He was here! Elijah! Right here!

Jezebel: Did you arrest him?

(Ahab smiles weakly.)

Jezebel: Fool! Must I do everything?

(Jezebel and Ahab mime arguing as Commentator speaks.)

Commentator 2: Well, a big blow struck by the God side, and the red team could have problems here. This drought could ruin the national economy.

(On the Elijah side, God beckons offstage, and a couple of Ravens flap onstage and deliver a loaf of bread and water bottle to Elijah, possibly by dropping them on his head.)

Commentator 1: Meanwhile, Elijah is doing all right over there with his coach, God, providing special energy food, delivered to him by Ravens. Well, the ball is now squarely in the red team's court. Round two.

Jezebel: Aghh! Right! I've had enough!

Ahab: *(Quaveringly, to the audience)* That's it. She's really mad. I can tell.

Jezebel: *(Fuming)* I want…I want…

Ahab: *(To the audience)* And she always gets what she wants.

Jezebel: Be quiet! I want the prophets of the Lord rounded up and killed. That'll show them who's boss around here.

Ahab: Yes, dear, we're the boss. *(Flinches.)* I mean, you are, really.

Commentator 1: Good heavens. A royal temper tantrum if I ever saw one. And Ahab is giving details to his army and servants. Things look bleak for the God team.

Commentator 2: Ahab calls Obadiah, his chief official.

Ahab: Obadiah.

(Obadiah stands forth from among the king's servants and supporters.)

Ahab: Any prophets in the local area—round them up and put them away!

Obadiah: Most assuredly, your majesty.

Commentator 1: But look at this. Here is a surprise move from the God team. It seems we actually have a God supporter on the red team. Interesting move.

(Obadiah goes across to God's prophets, beckons to them, and takes them safely somewhere on or offstage. He then returns, giving a thumbs up to God, who returns it.)

Commentator 2: And he's taking his orders to put away the true prophets quite literally. He's actually hiding them safely in a cave and providing them with food.

Commentator 1: So where's Elijah?

Commentator 2: He's out of the ring. In fact, he's using a clever avoidance tactic suggested by the coach. He's hiding far away in the wilderness.

Commentator 1: A clever psychological move. The drought is having its effect.

(Red team people mime being very hot and thirsty.)

Commentator 2: But look at the red team. Things are getting desperate there. Ahab is dying to hear the sound of rain. In fact, he's ordering his army to stand next to his palace and all spit on the roof at once.

(Ahab mimes giving orders and puts up an umbrella as the army spits.)

Commentator 1: But somehow it's just not the same.

Commentator 2: And here comes Jezebel. It's round three.

Jezebel: *(Fuming)* Aghhh! Everybody look here and listen. *(To Obadiah and troops)* Get out there and check again. If you find any of God's prophets left, kill them. But especially look for Elijah. He's the cause of all this.

(Soldiers leap offstage and go searching among the audience, congregating at the back of the venue. Obadiah stays on stage and wanders about, searching halfheartedly.)

Commentator 1: Well, there's a decisive move. The hunt is on for Elijah especially now, and I think the coach of the white team will have something to say.

Commentator 2: Yes, you're right.

(God and Elijah mime a conference.)

Commentator 2: God has decided that enough time has passed to soften up the opposition. God is now telling Elijah to go back to town, see the king, and tell him rain is on its way.

Commentator 1: And just look at Elijah's face. He's not happy about the idea of going back into town—and who can blame him with the queen on the warpath?

Jezebel: *(To Ahab)* Get him. This is your big chance. Don't mess it up. I'd do it myself, but I'm late for my facial appointment. *(She withdraws to the back section of the red team.)*

Ahab: *(Squares his shoulders and advances to center stage where Elijah is waiting.)* I will. I'll show him who's boss. *(Confronts Elijah with an effort at courage.)* Aha! There he is. The worst troublemaker in the whole land.

Elijah: *(Standing tall)* Don't give me that!

Ahab: No, er, of course not.

Elijah: You're the troublemaker. Not me. Filling the land with Baal worship from one end to the other! We'll soon see who's the true God around here. Bring out your prophets of Baal and all the false prophets your wife employs.

Ahab: *(Shuddering)* Oh no. Not them, too!

Elijah: Yes, them, too! And bring them out here so we can have a little contest. Tell all the people of Israel about it.

(Ahab returns to his false prophets and brings them to center stage. People of Israel enter and sit along the DS edge of the stage or in the audience. They cheer and gasp and point and carry on as the competition proceeds.)

Commentator 1: Now this is an interesting turn of events. A competition. What could Elijah and God be planning? It could be anything. And round four begins now.

Elijah: OK, you fakes. Build an altar to your precious Baal, and call on him to send down fire. Let's see what happens.

(The false prophets mime building and then dance wildly around their "altar" as Elijah stands to one side and the people of Israel gasp.)

Commentator 1: This is a move that requires Elijah to have absolute faith in his coach. If it comes off, it will be a king hit, but if it fails, it will be a disaster.

Commentator 2: And just look at those prophets of Baal dance.

(The prophets' dancing becomes frenzied. Ahab encourages them, obviously concerned by the lack of fire.)

Commentator 1: Well, it has been three hours now, and they've been at it solidly.

Elijah: Come on. Where's the fire, guys? Where's Baal? Maybe he's asleep, eh? Maybe he got sick of you guys and left the country.

Commentator 2: Wow, six hours. This is the longest religious aerobic session ever.

Commentator 1: But the crowd is getting restless. They've eaten their lunches already, and they're really looking for something to happen.

Elijah: *(Steps in to stop the action.)* All right. You've had your chance. Now stand back. *(Mimes building his altar.)* See? Altar! Wood! Meat! Water all over it and around it! Now! Oh Lord, please send fire and show us who's real.

(God races to Elijah's altar with a large red cloth and, with a thunderlike roar, places the red cloth around the altar. He then rushes back again.)

Commentator 2: Look at that! Fire falls from heaven. A king hit. Ahab is shocked.

Ahab: I'm shocked.

Commentator 1: And look at the reaction of the people.

(The people, who have been standing awestruck, now rush onto the stage, grab the false prophets, and rush them out through the audience or offstage.)

Commentator 2: Boy, I wouldn't want to be one of those false prophets.

Elijah: *(Striding up to Ahab, who cowers)* And as for you…

Ahab: Gulp!

Elijah: Go home and relax. Rain is on its way.

Ahab: *(In a tiny terrified voice)* But what will I tell the queen?

Elijah: That's your problem. She's your wife, not mine, thank heavens.

(Ahab slinks off, blubbering to himself. Elijah stands victorious DSC.)

Commentator 1: And so we have it, round four of this great tag team match.

Commentator 2: A massive victory for the God team.

Commentator 1: And the queen will not be impressed.

Jezebel: *(Advancing to the front of the red team to meet Ahab)* Well?

Ahab: Er, it's like this. You know your prophets of Baal…

Jezebel: Four hundred of them, yes.

Ahab: Well, they all got sort of…er…killed.

Jezebel: *(In a rage)* Aghh! Tell Elijah that if he isn't killed by tomorrow morning, I'm not the queen. I want him dead, dead, dead!

Ahab: That's pretty dead.

Jezebel: Be quiet, fool, and do it.

Ahab: Yes, of course, my petal. Er…soldiers, report here.

(Soldiers come rushing down from the back of the audience. Ahab mimes giving them instructions, gesturing madly. The soldiers immediately start searching through the audience for Elijah.)

Commentator 1: Well, this is a decisive start to round five. A search by the army for Elijah—and only Elijah. It will be interesting to see how Elijah handles this big challenge. And his reaction is…

(Elijah runs to his side.)

Commentator 1: …to run away.

Commentator 2: There he goes, all the way to the northern borders of Israel, as far as he can get, where he falls exhausted.

(Elijah collapses on the God side of the stage.)

Commentator 1: But his coach is being very sympathetic and letting him sleep it off.

Commentator 2: Elijah wakes somewhat refreshed by the rest, and his next reaction is…

(Elijah leaps up and runs again to upstage and back down to DS on the God team side, where he falls exhausted again.)

Commentator 2: …to run even farther away.

(God follows Elijah and stands over him.)

Commentator 2: But look at this. With a coach like God, you can't hide.

Commentator 1: God finds him in a cave on Mount Sinai.

God: Elijah, what are you doing here?

Elijah: I can't take any more. Jezebel has killed all your other prophets, and now she's after me with the whole army. You might as well kill me now.

God: Go back to Damascus. I'll show you who is to be king after Ahab dies.

Elijah: Go back?!

God: And by the way, you aren't the only supporter of mine left in Israel.

Elijah: *(Sarcastically)* Oh yeah? So who's the other one?

God: There are 7,000 of them.

Elijah: *(Coming off his high horse)* Oh. Right. *(Advances back to center stage.)*

Commentator 1: So what's going on back at the palace?

(Ahab steps forward, looking pleased with himself.)

Commentator 1: Ahab still hasn't gotten rid of those temples of Baal, and there's still plenty of Baal worshipping, too, even though the drought is over.

Commentator 2: And has Ahab improved?

(Ahab shakes his head and grins evilly.)

Commentator 2: No! There he goes, rampaging around.

(Ahab strides around the ring, grabs Naboth, pretends to slap him around, and has the soldiers drag him offstage.)

Commentator 1: Stealing people's possessions. Arranging murders with his evil queen— nothing's changed.

Commentator 2: But it can't last, and here's the reaction.

Elijah: *(Advances to Ahab, who is still having heaps of fun being evil.)* What do you think you're doing?

Ahab: Aghh! Are you still here?

Elijah: You think you can do what you like and walk all over people and steal their property. You've had your chance. You're doomed, and so is that so-called queen of yours.

(Ahab looks ready to collapse with fear.)

Commentator 1: And there's another big blow struck by the God team. But that's not all. Elijah strides out of the ring and tags Micaiah.

(Micaiah strides up to Ahab.)

Commentator 2: Micaiah's in, and the punishment just keeps coming.

Micaiah: The Lord will punish you. You'll die in the next battle you fight, and the queen will die soon after, just as Elijah said.

(Jezebel strides to the center and prods Ahab.)

Ahab: *(Taking encouragement from Jezebel)* Ha, ha! We'll see. Put him on bread and water till I return victorious.

(Ahab strides offstage as soldiers seize Micaiah.)

Jezebel: *(To the God team)* Forget it, guys! I'm boss, and don't you forget it.

Ahab: *(Returns with an arrow sticking out of his chest.)* Er...I don't feel so good. *(Ahab collapses.)*

Commentator 1: He would insist on fighting battles without the Lord's backing! *(Jezebel begins to look panicky.)*

Commentator 2: Jezebel is distraught. She doesn't know where to turn. She's putting on some moisturizer. Micaiah leaps out to tag Elisha. Elisha anoints Jehu as new king to replace Ahab.

(Elisha leaps onto stage, dragging Jehu after him. Jehu kneels, and Elisha anoints him. Jezebel looks more panicked. Jehu strides over to her.)

Commentator 1: Jezebel looks out the third-floor palace window to see if anyone is on her side. But some of her own servants push her out the window, and she splats.

(A couple of servants push Jezebel, and she "falls," which can be done dramatically if she runs backward offstage or through the audience, flailing her arms.)

Commentator 2: After all the warnings God gave her and Ahab, they still refused to take him seriously.

(Everyone on the white team side rejoices. Remaining members of red team come across to the white side and slap Elijah and the prophets on the back.)

Commentator 1: And there it is in six rounds. The God team still holds the title.

Commentator 2: In our next match, we'll see how Elisha tackles a series of invasions from enemy nations. Until then, it's goodnight.

(Blackout or curtain.)

Strain Your Brain, and Stretch Your Faith

Discuss as many of the following questions as time allows.

- **What risks did prophets such as Elijah and Micaiah face by standing up to the political establishment? How was Jesus in a similar situation?**

- **What are some modern examples of people doing this sort of thing?**

- **When have you found yourself in a similar situation?**

- **Even Elijah got scared and discouraged. When have you felt the same? Share the situation with the group if you want.**

- **How did God support and protect Elijah? How has God supported and protected you?**

- **When God found Elijah hiding, he didn't let the prophet stay there. God sent Elijah back into the field of battle, but with encouragement. What does this tell us about God? about ourselves?**

God, thank you for watching out for us and providing for us. Give us the courage and strength to stand up for you even against great odds. Take us onto your tag team, and coach us as we fight the good fight. And show us how to support each other as we work together to extend your kingdom. Amen.

The Good Samaritan
—The Director's Cut

And the Moral of the Story Is…
concern for others

Program Blurb:
The good, kind Samaritan rescues the poor man yet again, but will he be as kind as the script directs him to be?

What God Says: Luke 10:25-37

Handy Info: The parable has been told a million times, but still we need to ask ourselves, "Who is our neighbor?" and "How should we be good neighbors?"

Point out to your group that the Jerusalem to Jericho road was a known haunt of bandits; few people dared to travel it alone. A favorite trick of the bandits was to have one of them lie along the road looking like a bloodied victim. People of the time knew this, which is one reason the priest and the temple assistant didn't stop to help. The Samaritan, of course, was an unlikely hero for a Jewish audience because Jews despised Samaritans.

Props and Wardrobe:

You'll need a lectern, hammer and very large nails, and black eye makeup that can be smeared on quickly. You'll also need weapons, such as clubs and knives, for the bandits, as well as a machete and a power saw or chainsaw, with the blade or chain removed, that can be plugged in to run noisily. The Narrators should have scripts, or something that looks like a script, to read from.

The Narrators should wear nice clothes. The Samaritan, Priest, and Temple Assistant should wear Bible-times robes. The Thieves should wear something that suggests their occupation and carry weapons.

Groups that attack the Volunteer might wear team shirts or uniforms. The Volunteer needs to have clothing that looks perfectly normal in the audience but is easily removed, as well as T-shirt and shorts under his clothes.

Stage Manager's Clipboard:
Conceal a machete and power saw or chainsaw USC. (Be sure they can be plugged in somewhere.) Set a lectern on one downstage side, and put a hammer and the huge nails on it.

Cast List:

Narrators 1 and 2: totally concerned with completing this drama. They don't care about the suffering of the Volunteer; they just want a fill-in because neither of them wants the part.

Volunteer: a popular person, such as a youth leader or pastor, who is "spontaneously" chosen. The Volunteer should be male, as he gets beaten up a lot. He should not mind looking ridiculous on stage and should be physically well-coordinated.

Priest: very pompous and officious, might say the lines in a formal, chanting way, like a medieval monk

Temple Assistant: sanctimonious, self-righteous, very busy

Samaritan: excited about his own performance but ending up in conflict with the Narrators

Large reserve crowd of armed thieves and bandits and members of local sports teams or other groups

Someone recognizable to stride on stage and scare the thieves away

Cue: When the Volunteer is being beaten up by the mob, make sure the mob actors stand to make a solid wall but back a little from the Volunteer to give the Volunteer room to take off clothing and blacken his eye.

Cue: When the first Thieves attack, they can yell, but they must then "beat" the Volunteer silently to allow the Narrators' lines to be heard.

Cue: A circular saw or chainsaw with the blade or chain removed is a very safe but horrifyingly noisy instrument, and it looks *so* dangerous from the audience point of view. Still, safety first! Double-check everything before allowing teenagers to handle equipment.

The CD provides some fun audience cues for the Samaritan to hold up at the end to enhance his exit and further annoy the Narrators.

The Good Samaritan
—The Director's Cut

(The Volunteer is seated in the audience. Thieves and local sports team members are at the back of the audience. Narrator 1 enters briskly from any side and advances to lectern.)

Narrator 1: *(Reads)* Love your neighbor. "Who is my neighbor?" you may ask. Many parables deal with this question. One of them is that of the good Samaritan.

Once there was a man who was going on a journey from Jerusalem to Jericho. As he…

Narrator 2: *(Entering from same side but very determined.)* I'm *not* going to be the man.

Narrator 1: *(Pauses as if surprised.)* Why not?

Narrator 2: *(Evasively)* Oh, personal reasons. I just don't want to be the man, that's all.

Narrator 1: But we have to have someone be the man.

Narrator 2: *(Folds arms with determination and faces away from Narrator 1.)* Well, it's not going to be me. *(Turns to Narrator 1 with sudden inspiration.)* Why don't we use a member of the audience?

Narrator 1: *(Expresses exasperation, puts down script, and goes to Narrator 2 to negotiate.)* We can't use the audience. They're valuable. We need someone else.

Narrator 2: Hmm. He would have to be gullible.

Narrator 1: And slightly thick.

(The two suddenly hit on the same idea.)

Narrators 1 and 2: *(Smiling and beckoning to the Volunteer.)* You, there.

Volunteer: *(Leaping up in apparent amazement at being selected)* Yeah? Me?

Narrators 1 and 2: Yes. Come on. *(They continue with encouraging remarks as the Volunteer runs up onto stage excitedly.)*

Narrator 1: Now [name], you always wanted to be an actor, right?

(Volunteer agrees enthusiastically, almost childishly.)

Narrator 2: You haven't made it yet, right?

(Volunteer nods enthusiastically and then realizes what was said.)

Narrator 1: This could be your big break.

Volunteer: Yeah?

Narrator 2: Yes, for sure. I can see it now. Your name in lights 10 feet high. *(Holds arm out for effect and attempts to spell the Volunteers name but gets lost and gives up. Volunteer is mesmerized.)*

Volunteer: OK. I'm in. Let's do it.

Narrator 1: OK, now all you have to do is walk from here…*(pulls Volunteer across to the lectern side of the stage)* to there. *(Indicates the opposite side.)*

Volunteer: Yeah?

Narrator 2: *(Moving to lectern)* That's right. Can you handle that? Good.

(The two Narrators prepare to read the story. Volunteer stands in an exaggerated "ready to walk" posture, smiling and waving at the audience.)

Narrator 1: Once there was a man who was going on a long journey from Jerusalem to Jericho. As he…*(Notices that Volunteer hasn't started walking yet but is still waving at his "adoring public.")* Er, you can start now.

Volunteer: Now? Just like this? Just start?

(Narrators express some frustration as they gesture Volunteer to go. Volunteer exaggerates walking gait, smiling and waving all the time, thoroughly enjoying his moment of fame.)

Narrator 1: As he went, he was attacked by thieves.

(The Volunteer should reach the center of the stage at this point. Thieves suddenly roar and charge down the aisle. They drag the Volunteer upstage and surround him, apparently belting the daylights out of him. The Narrators stand calmly while all this is going on.

The Volunteer, screened from the audience by the thieves, rips off his shirt, pants, shoes, and socks and blackens his eye. Thieves can grab clothes as they come off and throw them over their shoulders for better effect.)

Narrator 2: And they were joined by [insert name of group].

(Members of a local sports team or other notable group come roaring down the aisle to join the fun onstage.)

Narrator 1: And by [insert name].

(Another local group races down to help beat up the Volunteer.)

Narrator 2: They beat him up, took his clothes, and left him half dead by the road.

Narrator 1: (To Narrator 2) I think that might be enough now.

Narrator 2: I think so, too.

Narrator 1: And in the end, they were all scared off by [insert name].

(The popular figure strides onto the stage. The mob takes one look and runs off screaming. The local character chases them.

The Volunteer is left in a mess at the back of the stage. He rises with difficulty, wanders DSC, and collapses in a heap.)

Narrator 2: (Calling to Volunteer) Well? How was that?

Volunteer: (In a broken voice) I'm half dead!

Narrator 1: Well, don't worry. Someone will come along and help in a bit.

(Volunteer makes a broken gurgling to signify that he is pleased to hear this news.)

Narrator 2: Along that road there came a priest.

Priest: (Enters grandly from side opposite lectern, chanting as he walks) Oh, I'm a good priest, a nice priest, a holy priest, and a very modest priest.

Narrator 1: He saw the man by the side of the road.

Priest: (Exaggerates a "stop and look" move and continues to chant) Oh, look, a man lying by the side of the road. He's all dirty and smelly…

Volunteer: (Chanting on the same note) And half dead.

Priest: (Chanting) Does this hurt? (Gives the Volunteer a swift kick. Volunteer yells.)

Volunteer: A bit.

Priest: (Chanting again) Oh, well. I'd better be getting along to the temple.

Narrator 2: But aren't you going to help him?

Priest: Sorry, I gave to the Red Cross already this year. (Exits.)

Volunteer: (Incensed) He didn't help!

Narrator 1: Don't worry. Someone else will be along. They'll be sure to help.

(Volunteer slumps back to the floor, obviously not convinced.)

Narrator 2: And next along the road there came a temple assistant.

Temple Assistant: (*Enters from side of stage opposite lectern, talking to himself and counting on his fingers.*) First, I'll polish the seven-branched candlesticks. Then I'll polish the bronze doors. Then I'll polish the sacrificial cows. Then I'll…(*Walks straight into the Volunteer, who emits another loud groan or yell.*)

Oh, look. Someone lying by the side of the road all covered in dirt and muck. (*Begins lecturing, wagging his finger and shaking his fist.*) It's people like you who are an obstacle to transport. Why don't you get a job? Get a haircut. Get a bath. And stop blocking the road! (*Exits.*)

Volunteer: He didn't help either!

Narrator 1: Um, well, there is one more person. I'm sure…

Volunteer: Yeah, I know. (*Singsong*) Nobody helps the man by the road…

Narrator 2: Oh, be quiet. And along the road there came a Samaritan and his donkey.

(*Samaritan enters from side opposite lectern and mimes dragging with difficulty what is obviously a very stubborn and unwilling donkey.*)

Narrator 1: The Samaritan was a despised and rejected person.

Narrator 2: Everyone hated him.

Narrator 1: He was slimy…

Narrator 2: And grimy…

Narrator 1: (*Starting to enjoy it, even as the Samaritan is getting sick of it*) And ugly…

Narrator 2: And dumb…

Samaritan: All right! Don't push it!

Narrator 2: He saw the man.

Samaritan: (*Stops short. Flings up both hands and points.*) Look! A man!

Narrator 1: His heart was filled with pity.

(*Samaritan screams, tears his hair, throws himself into the lap of someone in the audience, and rolls on the floor.*)

Narrator 1: (*Interrupting*) I said his heart was filled with pity, not that he was a raving emotional wreck!

(*Samaritan instantly stops and goes grumpily back to the stage.*)

Narrator 2: He went over to the man and helped him.

(*Samaritan evidently doesn't want to cooperate now that his acting didn't get a response. His unwillingness to do anything to help becomes more and more obvious.*)

Narrator 2: He poured oil on the poor man's wounds.

(*Samaritan mimes taking a bottle out of the donkey's side pack. It is evidently hot. He gingerly handles it and pours something onto the man, who yells. Someone on an offstage microphone can make a sizzling sound if you like.*)

Narrator 1: (*Frustrated*) Not boiling oil! Medicinal oil!

Narrator 2: And he poured wine on the wounds.

(*Samaritan mimes taking a bottle out of the donkey's side pack and drinking from it.*)

Narrator 1: On the *wounds*!!

(*Samaritan gives Narrators an annoyed look and then splashes a bit of wine on the Volunteer.*)

Narrator 2: And he bandaged the wounds.

(*Samaritan mimes taking a very long bandage from the pack and commences to wind it around and around the Volunteer starting at his feet and going up to his head as if making him a mummy. Volunteer stiffens his arms and legs close to his body and wriggles to give the impression of being tied up.*

Samaritan then mimes taking the long loose end of the bandage and flinging it over a low-hanging branch nearby and hauling on it. Working in time with the arm movements of the Samaritan, the Volunteer raises his feet until, with his hands under his hips, he is lying with his legs vertical, looking as if he is tied up to a tree branch. The Samaritan ties off the bandage and looks triumphantly and defiantly at the Narrators.)

Narrator 1: *(Thoroughly annoyed at the Samaritan's defiance.)* Look at that! What are you doing? Get him down now! You'll hold up the drama.

(The Samaritan slowly wanders upstage to get the large machete. Volunteer makes muffled noises of distress. The Samaritan, with a dramatic slicing movement, cuts the bandage that is suspending the Volunteer, who crashes onto the floor, still tied up. Samaritan stands looking in defiant unconcern toward the Narrators, hands on hips.)

Narrator 2: Well, go on. Get rid of all the bandages.

(With a giant sigh, the Samaritan wanders back to upstage to get the chainsaw and revs it with evident delight. The Volunteer wriggles in fear as he sees what is happening. The Samaritan advances deliberately toward the Volunteer and begins to mime cutting through the bandages, going along each arm from the hand up. The Volunteer realizes that he is being cut free. He is able to sit up and seems quite grateful. His mouth is cut free so he can move his face. Then the Samaritan starts on the legs, beginning at one foot. Volunteer goes rigid and yells as the saw gets closer and at the final point stops dead just short of tragedy. The rigid Volunteer collapses on the floor. The Samaritan gives the Narrators a "satisfied now?" look and stands waiting for instructions.)

Narrator 1: That's better. He picked up the poor man and put him on his donkey.

(Samaritan starts to bend down but is interrupted.)

Narrator 2: Now, remember, when you lift, bend the knees.

(Samaritan roughly grabs the Volunteer's knees and pulls them up to bent. The Volunteer yells.)

Narrator 1: Not his knees! Yours!

(Samaritan grabs the Volunteer by the hair and pulls him up, flings him over the donkey. The Volunteer allows himself to be pulled up and ends up standing bent double, as if touching his toes.)

Narrator 2: And he took the poor man to an inn.

(Samaritan and the Volunteer travel toward the opposite side of stage from lectern. Samaritan leads his donkey along slowly, and the Volunteer shuffles his feet in little sideways steps to follow still bent over the donkey.)

Narrator 1: When they got to the inn…

Samaritan: We're not there yet.

(Narrators express frustration as Samaritan and Volunteer move slowly to the opposite side of the stage and stop.)

Narrator 1: When they got to the inn…

Samaritan: Not yet. We're there, but we're not at peace. We have to be at peace.

> *(Narrators look exasperated while the Samaritan breathes deeply and finally looks peaceful. He grabs the Volunteer by the hair, lifts his head up roughly, and yells.)* Are you at peace? *(Volunteer moans, and Samaritan drops Volunteer's head again.)* We're at peace now.

Narrator 2: *(Stifling a groan)* When they got to the inn, the Samaritan said to the innkeeper, "Here are two silver coins."

Samaritan: *(Addressing the audience)* Here is one silver coin.

Narrator 1: Two!

Samaritan: Here are two plastic coins.

Narrator 2: Silver!

Samaritan: *(With a sigh of boredom)* Here are two silver coins.

Narrator 1: Take care of him…

Samaritan: *(Suddenly breaking into hugely dramatic Shakespearean expression, realizing that this is his final line)* Take care of him…

Narrator 2: And when I return…

Samaritan: *(Still gesturing madly)* and when I return…

Narrator 1: I will pay…

Samaritan: I will pay…

Narrator 2: All my money to the Narrators.

Samaritan: All my money to…*(Stops and looks at Narrators impatiently.)*

Narrator 1: Sorry, just our little joke. I will pay anything else I owe you.

Samaritan: I will pay anything else I owe you.

Narrator 2: There. That's it. You can bow.

(Samaritan goes into a frenzy of bowing, blowing kisses, and shaking hands with members of the audience. Narrators show frustration. Narrators walk across to the Volunteer, now lying in a heap.)

Narrator 1: Well, how was that?

(Volunteer emits a gurgle.)

Narrator 2: You can go, too.

Volunteer: I couldn't walk a step.

Narrator 1: *(To Narrator 2)* Oh, good. While we're here, we could do the Crucifixion scene.

(The Volunteer's head shoots up with a horrified facial expression. He watches in terror as the Narrators happily race over to the lectern and produce a hammer and some enormous nails. Despite his injuries, he runs as they charge toward him.

Curtain or blackout.)

Strain Your Brain, and Stretch Your Faith

Discuss as many of the following questions as time allows.

- **Jesus made a number of points in this parable. One is about being helpful to others. What is another?**
- **Have you passed by someone who needed help? Explain.**
- **How does society discourage people from helping others?**
- **People who need help are often not packaged attractively. What are some examples of this?**

Have participants from groups of four to write a modern version of the story. Help the groups stay focused on the unexpected helper and being inclusive.

PRAY

Lord Jesus, we are surrounded by need and distress, not only material but emotional and spiritual as well. Awaken us to the cries of help around us, and open our hearts and eyes to hear and see the silent cries of those who are too angry, frustrated, or frightened to make their needs known. Give us the courage to stop and help, and forgive us when we pass by on the other side of the road. Amen.

Make Me a Belief

And the Moral of the Story Is...

faith, human nature, syncretism

Program Blurb:

A customer comes to a "philosophy shop" to have a custom-made philosophy designed. Like so many people in a secular society, the customer ends up with contradictory ideas cobbled together from several philosophies and religions, excluding, of course, Christianity (who'd want that?).

What God Says: Acts 17:16-34; 1 Corinthians 1:18-29; Colossians 4:6

Handy Info:

Use this drama for an older youth group coming to grips with philosophical and theological ideas. The humor comes from contradictions within the "system," which is tacked together for a customer who, in the end, admits to not wanting to commit to anything that will impose any real changes in his or her life. In the Western world, syncretism (the tendency to bring together different aspects and strands of varying belief systems and combine them) is the result of the popular notion of being tolerant and not exclusive. Many times Christians are put down as having too narrow a view of what is right and wrong. It is very easy to disguise unwillingness to stand up for anything under a mantle of "Well, after all, what is right and wrong anyway? I take a more open view." (Translated, "I'll believe anything that saves me doing what doesn't suit me.")

Christianity also goes against modern thinking because it takes the individual out of the driver's seat and puts God there. That isn't a popular option in a society where people think, "Hey, it's your life. You do anything you like, and if it's OK for you, then it's OK."

Props and Wardrobe: You'll need a mirror and a table for the counter. If you want the Customer to put on items of clothing to represent the different ideas, you'll need an assortment of mismatched items that can be layered easily.

Both the Customer and the Salesperson begin the skit in ordinary clothes.

Stage Manager's Clipboard:

The CD provides "belief system" labels that can be printed out and taped onto the Customer. Use these labels by themselves or with the assorted clothing items. When the Salesperson summarizes all the features of the Customer's philosophy, he or she can tear off part of the HINDUISM and BUDDHISM labels to make the point that the Customer only wants part of these beliefs.

Cast List:

The Customer: likes to think of himself or herself as a deep thinker but really knows very little and doesn't really want to get involved

The Salesperson: businesslike and showing little emotion but certainly more educated and aware of things than the customer is

Cue: The more ridiculous the Customer looks at the end, the better the mismatched appearance symbolizes what happens when incongruous beliefs are tacked together.

Cue: Make sure the use of clothes and labels doesn't slow the action or you'll lose the audience. If you use mismatched clothes, choose things that are easy to put on, such as hats, gloves, loose pants, or shawls.

Make Me a Belief

(Customer enters shop from either side of stage. Salesperson is waiting behind the counter.)

Customer: Good morning. I'd like a belief system—some set of ideas that will fit the way I want to live.

Salesperson: Well, we have a few on special today. How about this one—anti-intellectual pragmatism? You know, "Anyone who thinks about things is weird." You just do what works and get on with it.

Customer: Um, no, I'd like it to sound more educated. I want to look like I've thought it all out. How about that one? What's that?

Salesperson: That's called secular humanism. It's been popular for a couple of hundred years.

Customer: What is it?

Salesperson: Oh, it's good for those who want to believe we have it all together. You know, ultimate confidence in human progress. No God or supernatural stuff.

Customer: Hey, I like that. It has a gutsy, independent feel. Who needs religion for a crutch? I'm a modern scientific person.

Salesperson: Ah, then you could add some of this—scientism. It pushes science beyond purely scientific study of the universe. You use it to try to explain ultimates, like the existence of God, which science isn't equipped to handle, but still…*(Shrugs.)*

Customer: OK, but I don't want to look naive. I want to look a little cautious about the future.

Salesperson: We'll add a touch of modern pessimism. And what about some environmentalism? Then you can look concerned about the natural world.

Customer: Lovely. But I don't want to sound touchy-feely. I mean, I'm not some hippy dropout. I'm a person of action. I want to be part of the real world. I want to build a successful career. I want to struggle and survive and rise.

Salesperson: Well, how about a drop or two of social Darwinism—the struggle for existence, the strong succeed as the weak fall by the wayside? *(With sudden inspiration)* Hey! You can claim to be an aggressive type-A person. That will justify trampling other people underfoot.

Customer: Yes, but I don't want to be unpopular. I want the human touch, or else men *(or women if it's a male actor)* won't be attracted to me.

Salesperson: OK, well, we'll disguise that with a veneer of old-fashioned philanthropism.

Customer: What?

Salesperson: Oh, giving money to charities on television.

Customer: I see. *(Looks in mirror.)* OK, that's looking good so far. But I've been thinking about the secular humanism thing. I mean, I don't necessarily want absolutely *no* possibility of a God. I want to be able to call for help in a tight spot. You know, maybe I should save something for a rainy day.

Salesperson: Like when you die?

Customer: That's it.

Salesperson: Then you need theism.

Customer: What?

Salesperson: Theism—a belief in some sort of active god.

Customer: *(Suspiciously)* Is it socially acceptable?

Salesperson: Oh, yes, provided you select the right type and don't get too involved. How about Christian theism—a loving creator God who comes and dies to save us?

Customer: Oh no, not that. That Christian stuff's not real. Jesus probably didn't even exist. I saw this show on television that proved it. And who believes the Bible nowadays? I've never bothered to read it.

Salesperson: OK, so we'll start with critical rejection based on the mass media.

Customer: But I want to sound like I've thought about it.

Salesperson: Oh. *(Quickly thinking of a good term)* Well, we'll call it postmodern skepticism.

Customer: Oh, that's nice.

Salesperson: Tell you what—you can say you're a free thinker. Not interested in churchy doctrines. And you are not a theist but a deist; you believe in a god that never gets involved in the world.

Customer: Look, can we make it sound a bit mystical. *(Concerned)* I don't want to get too specific with this God stuff. Something vague that I can keep at arm's length.

Salesperson: Well, we could try some pantheism, the idea that God is the universe itself. There's the Hindu type, Brahman—the distant God too abstract for us to relate to.

Customer: Yes, I want the Indian one. The East is sort of…well…spiritual.

Salesperson: Good. Some Hindu pantheism. Now which Hindu path to enlightenment do you want to pursue—jnana yoga, karma yoga, bhakti, shaktism, tantric cults?

Customer: I don't know. I just want something Hindu.

Salesperson: Oh. Well, how about some hatha yoga? That's popular in the West, and you can just use it as exercises if you want.

Customer: Does it mean I go to nirvana when I die?

Salesperson: Uh, nirvana? That's Buddhism.

Customer: But I like the idea of nirvana, like a sort of heaven.

Salesperson: No, nirvana isn't a place. It is a state of mind, and ultimately it is nothingness. Complete freedom from everything. You cease to exist. Blank. Gone.

Customer: Oh. But I like the word *(savoring it)* nirvanaaaa. It has a mystical ring.

Salesperson: You could try popular village Buddhism. They have lots of heavens.

Customer: Yes, that's the sort of nirvana I mean.

Salesperson: How about we throw in a couple of overseas trips to Southeast Asia? You could shop in Singapore, stay in the Bangkok Hilton, visit a few temples, and then say it was a spiritual pilgrimage.

Customer: *(Really liking the idea)* I could say I definitely felt a sense of something.

Salesperson: But to stay on the safe side, you could say you are an agnostic, unconvinced by any evidence for or against a god.

Customer: Great. I want to look tolerant. I don't want to be accused of being exclusive. I mean, all religions are the same in the end.

Salesperson: You can quote Ramakrishna.

Customer: Who's he?

Salesperson: The Hindu sage who said all religions are valid.

Customer: Oh, OK. I mean, after all, it's a democratic right to believe what I want. No one can come around and preach to me. I decide what I believe. I'll fight for that.

But, of course, in the end there's no such thing as right and wrong. As long as you're sincere.

Salesperson: Ah, relativism, no absolutes. That will cover it all nicely and justify everything. With this, you can accept virtually anything and never be accused of being narrow-minded or exclusive.

Customer: Great. Let's see how it all looks.

Salesperson: Right. *(Listing all the features in combination.)* You are a secular humanist, and you deny Christianity and Jesus and reject the Bible, which you haven't read. You have confidence in the progress of modern science, and you glory in the achievements of humankind, but you have a sense of crisis about the future. You are an environmentalist who values the natural world. *(Pauses.)*

Ah. Now that could be linked to Christian ideas of the gift of a created world. We'll have to ignore that connection.

Customer: Right.

Salesperson: You are a social Darwinian wanting to be involved in the free enterprise struggle, but you embrace some convenient bits of charitable philanthropism. *(Aside)* Now we'll have to ignore the fact that philanthropism is based on the Christian idea of the value of other humans. *(Back to the list)* You believe in an indefinable something, like a pantheistic Hindu Brahma presence, *but* you are also skeptical and agnostic, *but* you still want something to be there in case you die. *(Reconsidering)* However, you won't want the rest of Hinduism because it suggests that the world is an illusion. Now that could clash with your wanting to be an environmentalist. OK. *(Plunging on)* You like the idea of going to nirvana but not the rest of Buddhism because it says you should detach yourself from the world and that

could threaten your career path. But none of it matters, anyway, because all religions are OK…

Customer: *(Interrupting)* Except Christianity.

Salesperson: …Right. You want to look educated and like you've considered all angles, but you won't have anyone preach to you. And finally there's no such thing as right and wrong, but you'll fight for your right to believe what you want because that's the right thing. Phew. How's that?

Customer: I guess so.

Salesperson: What do you mean, you guess so? This is your whole approach to life here. This is what drives your behavior and attitudes, the way you treat others, the way you see yourself. Do you believe it, or don't you?

Customer *(Looks from side to side and then leans forward and speaks in a tense stage whisper.)* Look, I don't actually want to get involved. I have a comfortable life here, and I don't want to change. Will this package protect me or not?

Salesperson: Oh, yes. With this package, you can simply go on living a Western consumer-based lifestyle in total comfort. No feelings that you might be missing out on something. You can completely avoid having to consider any deeper issues.

Customer: Great. I'll take it. What's it cost?

Salesperson: What?

Customer: Well, I will have to pay for this, won't I?

Salesperson: *(With a slightly ominous tone)* Oh, yes, you'll pay for it all right. 'Bye.

(Customer gives a quizzical look and then exits. Blackout or curtain.)

Strain Your Brain, and Stretch Your Faith

Discuss as many of the following questions as time allows. Have your group form small groups of three or four. Allow a few minutes for discussion after you ask each question, and then ask for volunteers to share insights from the small-group discussion.

- **What is the customer looking for?**

- **What does the salesperson construct for the customer?**

- **Why is there so much of this sort of confused thinking in today's society?**

- **How can Christians stand up for what they believe in a non-arrogant and sensitive manner?**

- **Is it all right for Christians to agree with aspects or teachings of a non-Christian religion or philosophy?**

- **What is the meaning of the salesperson's last line?**

- **It has been said of faith sharing that no one was ever argued into heaven. What does this mean, and what are its implications?**

- **Christianity itself is a profound theological and philosophical proposition with many deeply meditative ideas and areas of mystery. Why is it so often presented in the media as shallow and materialistic? How can we plumb some of these deeps for ourselves?**

God, thank you for the marvel of your own presence with us. Thank you for the endless mystery that you are, which we can only begin to understand. Thank you also for coming to us, walking our earth, and being with us.

We are surrounded by many ideas and religions. In all our dealings with those who believe differently, make us patient, loving, and humble, but make us strong and forthright in the way we stand up for you. Grant us your Holy Spirit as we share the good news of your love for everyone. Amen.

Topical Index

Scripture Index